RELIGION AND POLITICAL SOCIETY

A HARPER FORUM BOOK

RELIGION AND POLITICAL SOCIETY

Jürgen Moltmann

Herbert W. Richardson

Johann Baptist Metz

Willi Oelmüller

M. Darrol Bryant

Edited and Translated in
The Institute of Christian Thought

HARPER & ROW, PUBLISHERS
NEW YORK, EVANSTON, SAN FRANCISCO, LONDON

The chapters by J. B. Metz, Jürgen Moltmann, and Willi Oelmüller are translated from *Kirche im Prozess der Aufklärung*. Copyright © 1970 by Chr. Kaiser Verlag and Matthias-Grünewald-Verlag. RELIGION AND POLITICAL SOCIETY. Copyright © 1974 by Harper & Row, Publishers, Inc. All rights reserved. Printed in the United States of America. No part of this book may be used or reproduced in any manner whatsoever without written permission except in the case of brief quotations embodied in critical articles and reviews. For information address Harper & Row, Publishers, Inc., 10 East 53rd Street, New York, N.Y. 10022. Published simultaneously in Canada by Fitzhenry & Whiteside Limited, Toronto.

FIRST EDITION

Library of Congress Cataloging in Publication Data
Main entry under title:

Religion and political society.

(A Harper forum book)
Includes bibliographical references.
1. Christianity and politics—Addresses, essays, lectures. 2. Eschatology—Addresses, essays, lectures. 3. Religion and sociology—Addresses, essays, lectures. I. Moltmann, Jürgen. II. Institute of Christian Thought.
BR115.P7R434 1974   261.7   73-18424
ISBN 0-06-065564-X

To J. Edgar Bruns

Contents

Preface

In response to the political upheavals of the late 1960s, three German theologians collaborated in the preparation of a programmatic volume dealing with the relation between religion and politics. Its thesis was that the Enlightenment conceptions of rationality and freedom should be revived as principles for guiding political philosophy and theology today. The Enlightenment tradition gives centrality to the activity of criticism. In the eighteenth century Enlightenment, critical reason was directed against dogmatic images of nature and religion; in the nineteenth century Enlightenment, critical reason was directed against conservative notions of art, economics, and society. Kant, Hegel, and Marx are the heroes of this Enlightenment tradition.

In their programmatic volume, Metz, Moltmann, and Oelmüller interpreted the activity of critical reason as a freeing, or liberating, power. They argued that the ideas of the Enlightenment have worked within history to free humanity. The history of the Enlightenment tradition is, therefore, claimed to be a *Freiheitsgeschichte* —a history of the freeing of mankind.

The reason why Metz, Moltmann, and Oelmüller urge the revitalization of Enlightenment ideas in modern thought is that they see an analogy between the Enlightenment concept of freedom and the Christian freedom that is proclaimed by St. Paul. The Christian gospel, too, generates a *Freiheitsgeschichte*. Moreover, they see an analogy between the Enlightenment notion of criticism and the biblical opposition to all idolatry, all finite absolutes. Christian faith, too, generates a tradition of criticism. The programmatic point of the German volume was the affirmation that

Christian and Enlightenment conceptions of criticism and freedom should be systematically interrelated in order to create a
theology of politics. In this way, religion and political society
could be conceived to be working together in an organic way.
In developing their new theory, the German theologians attempted
to go beyond both contemporary radical and conservative theories
of politics. For this reason, they engaged in debate with a variety
of contemporary theoretical alternatives: Karl Popper, Max
Horkheimer, Robert Bellah, Karl Deutsch, and others.

Because of the intrinsic importance of their proposal, as well
as the widespread interest in the relation between religion and
political society in North America today, it was decided to make
the Metz-Moltmann-Oelmüller volume the focus of a program
of study at the Institute of Christian Thought (a graduate faculty
and research center, located in Toronto, which includes both
Catholic and Protestant theologians of several national back-
grounds). In the course of this study, the German volume was
translated and edited by a working group. In addition, two essays
attempting to develop further the original thesis and show its
relevance to the North American situation were prepared and
added to the collection. The result is the present volume.

The members of the working group are Darrol Bryant, Thomas
Hughson, David Kelly, Joan Lockwood, Herbert W. Richardson,
Paul Rigby, and Henry Vander Goot. Those primarily responsible
for specific translations, introductions, or notes are named at
appropriate places within the volume. However, the work has
been engaged in cooperatively throughout.

We wish especially to thank Professor Barbara Carvill of the
University of Toronto for her assistance with the German translations. She has worked wonders to improve our endeavors; we, of
course, are still responsible for the errors remaining.

Finally, we have omitted many of the footnotes and references
that accompanied the original German essays. Some of these
dealt specifically with the German situation and are not usefully
reproduced here. Others were references to works available only
in German and hence not accessible to readers of this English
edition. Those scholars wishing this information will, of course,
prefer to work in the original German text where the full ap-

paratus is to be found.* The present volume is not identical with, nor intended as a substitute for, that work.

Toronto
Easter 1974

* *Kirche im Prozess der Aufklärung.* München: Chr. Kaiser Verlag. Mainz: Matthias-Grünewald-Verlag. 1970.

RELIGION AND POLITICAL SOCIETY

Introduction

Herbert W. Richardson

The methodological principle governing these essays is the primacy of criticism. The theological principle is the rejection of every identification of utopian thinking with Christian eschatology.

Why criticism? Because it is a possible antidote to the two dominant tendencies in modern politics, tendencies that today are actually destroying politics. These two tendencies are ideology and systems-thinking.

Ideology, in the strict sense of the term, is a world view generated to provide a rationale for an existing state of society. What all ideologies have in common is their attempt to suppress contradictions both in society and in thought about society. Ideology seeks to conceive the existing world as rational and, therefore, as already being a system. An ideology is a rationalization of a state of affairs that is not rational, but to some extent irrational. The effect of an ideology is, therefore, to suppress contradiction and discontent and, ipso facto, political conflict and compromise.

The original analysis of ideology by Karl Marx did not, however, discover a way to go beyond ideology. Marx saw that early capitalist societies generated a total system of ideas which functioned to make people blind to the actual contradictions in the society. In this way, the ideology justified the status quo. Marx sought to expose this ideology by a consistent critique of society; but by virtue of its very consistency (i.e., the judgment that the economic factor is always determinative of every institution within the society), Marx's critique became itself an ideology. Marx's analysis itself construed society as a system and made its adherents blind to the diversity of interests and institutions actually at work. Marx's analysis itself presupposed, as the basis of political engagement, the idea of a future society that would be without contradictions and radical diversity. Hence, the Marxist call for revolution and its attempt to create political opposition within society does not rest on a *political* vision of society, but upon an ideological conviction that politics is, in the last analysis, dispensable.

We shall see in what follows that the ideological character of Marxism and its ultimate rejection of politics derives from its identification of utopian thinking with eschatology. For the Marxist, the only heaven there is is the heaven man can create on earth. For this reason, then, both conservative and revolutionary ideologies have certain traits in common. Both those who affirm the present state of society as essentially harmonious and those who oppose it in the name of some total new future assume that society can be a harmonious unitary structure. They assume that a society's institutions reinforce one another and are governed by the same principle of order and activity.

For example, according to the dominant American ideology, the several institutions of society—family, school, state, business, church, etc.—are affirmed to be "separate," but assumed to be complementary. To suggest that their interests are not rationally harmonizable and complementary is to undercut the basic presupposition that America is one social structure: one people united in terms of one civil religion (or set of values). To affirm that America is one social structure includes also the idea that one principle of order and activity is alike at work in every particular institution, namely, the "democratic ideal," the ideal of "freedom." Why, in America, is it thought desirable that the school, the family, the Church, the state, and the world of commerce and industry should all operate on "democratic principles"? Because these institutions are all regarded as *functions* of one social system or structure and, therefore, as properly moved and ordered by *its* dominant values and mechanisms.

The conventional analysis of American society is, in fact, not formally different from a Marxist interpretation. The Marxist would also presuppose that American society is a system, but would affirm that the controlling principle of that system is the profit motive and economic domination. In the Marxist view, every institution within a capitalist society itself functions in terms of the profit motive. The family, the school, the state, the Church are all instruments of economic exploitation and domination. What the Marxist interpretation has in common with the liberal American interpretation is that they both presuppose society to be a system of interlocking institutions governed by the same principle of order and activity. Because of this presupposition, both interpretations become *ideological*; that is, both become interpretations that suppress the actual plurality, diversity, and contradiction among institutions and actions in the interests of providing a total rational account of human behavior. Because both Marxist and American interpretations of society deny or disparage the genuine plurality of interests and types of institutions in a society, they both regard politics (which presupposes plurality) as dispensable. They both aspire to develop a scientific theory of society and to administer society sociotechnically. This is why both theories become apologists for the most characteristic institution of the modern world: bureaucracy.

All the essays in this volume regard totalism, whether in theory or in practice, as the most dangerous threat to the existence of humane life today. Theoretical totalism is ideology; practical totalism is bureaucracy—the organization of life in terms of the principle of sameness. Ideology implies total social system, and total social system implies bureaucracy and the reduction of the plurality of institutions and life. To argue, as some Marxists do, that society is a social system organized for the sake of economic exploitation—so that the method for overcoming this injustice is but the socialization of the means of production—leads not to freedom, but to bureaucracy. To argue, as some Americans do, that human freedom is best preserved by maintaining a market economy and a market economy press ("competition of free speech and advertising") leads not to freedom, but to bureaucracy. All *ideological* political programs lead to an augmentation of the power of the total state precisely because ideology presupposes that society is not composed of a plurality of separate and incommensurate interests, but is, rather, a single system. (It is worth noting, too, that contemporary sociology—to the extent that it presupposes society is a single functional system—tends to reinforce the ideological tendency of modern political theory.)

The danger to politics today, argue the essays in this volume, arises from the attempt to unify and systematize what is actually plural and unsystematizable. The danger arises from the attempt to create a "science" of politics, an ideological rationale for action, a structuralist interpretation of society. All such efforts obscure the plurality of institutions, interests, and agents as well as their unsystematizable diversity and conflict. It is precisely because of this diversity and conflict that society cannot be humanely ordered by ideology or sociotechnics, but only by politics. Politics is not a science and not a theology. Politics is, rather, a practical enterprise devoted to creating a contingent and ever-changing order by compromising and balancing diverse and competing interests against one another. This conception of politics is particularly discussed by Willi Oelmüller in his essay "The Limitations of Social Theories." In analyzing the assumptions of three contemporary social theories, Oelmüller makes clear how a scientific account of society can only be given by overlooking the diversity of situations and the plurality of human freedoms. The essay "What Makes a Society Political?" further argues for the notion that politics is a *sui generis* type of social order that can only be created through the clash of contrary and unharmonizable interests which are, finally, compromised in contingent, revisable arrangements.

Still, the predominance of ideological thinking in our time (as well as the primacy of the sociological method of interpreting behavior) has actually led to the loss of the idea of politics. How can this idea be recovered? How can politics be restored? The thinkers in this volume argue, more or less explicitly, that the beginning of political thinking is *criticism*. It is criticism that shows the limitation of all totalistic accounts of human life. It is criticism that reveals the true diversity of human life. Human beings attain to genuine freedom and understanding only as they eschew total theories and lay hold on the power of reason *to criticize every idea of the whole, every notion of the absolute.*

To be reasonable and free means, therefore, not to divinize the human condition, but to determine its limitations and set its proper boundaries. Criticism is the act of locating man in his world as a finite being and regarding his political endeavors not as "building the kingdom of God here on earth," but as the creation of a tenuous finite good: a house to live in, a state that is at peace. This conception of criticism is, argue Moltmann and Oelmüller, our heritage from the Enlightenment. And this conception of criticism is also the political expression of faith in the God who cannot be known by any idea, but only through faith. In "The Cross and Civil Religion," Moltmann affirms the continuity of faith in the cross and the act of critical limitation of the claims of all human theories and powers.

The second point on which the writers of this volume concur is their opposition to any identification of utopian thinking with Christian eschatology. This opposition is specifically directed against modern theologians who have identified these two and sought to reinterpret the Christian teaching about man's ultimate fulfillment as a teaching about a future utopian society.

Utopian thinking has been an essential ingredient in modern political thought. It has functioned to give us an idealized image of the future, an image in terms of which we cannot only criticize present society, but also determine positive directions for change. Utopian thinking emerges in conjunction with modern philosophies of history, that is, in conjuction with those philosophies that attempt to interpret human history as a process moving towards some future perfected society or social goal. Philosophies of history play the same role in our time as philosophies of being played in the Middle Ages. Medieval philosophies of being provided a total scheme of human existence according to which everything was "higher" or "lower." This "chain of being" had its peak in a supernatural heaven that was attained by mystical experience and by the immortality of the soul after death. Modern philosophies of history, on the other hand, provide a total scheme in which everything is either "earlier" or "later" in history. This "chain of history" has its culmination in a future society that is attained by ideological action and social involvement.

Philosophies of being and philosophies of history are both

totalistic. Both construe the meaning of life within a single rational continuum and affirm, thereby, the ultimacy of the order in which we live. There is no room in either for the possibility of the impossible: the Pascalian wager, the Kierkegaardian leap, the resurrection from the dead. On such views, the world does not contain contraries; it is an immanent system. Man's reason (according to both philosophies) does not entertain as true any contradictions or radical pluralities. Man's reason (according to both) is not political. Man's reason becomes instead a technical instrument for maintaining the order of the system and instructing him in behavior consistent with it.

Utopian thinking emerges as the lynchpin of every philosophy of history because utopian thinking determines the horizon of thought and action. At first, utopian thinking may actually be a ferment and a goad to social criticism. But eventually, even utopian thinking operates as part of the closed-system philosophy of history that limits the possibilities of human life to those which are rationally systematizable within its scheme. When man confuses his thoughts about a utopian future with thoughts about a future beyond every utopia, he loses the possibility of transcending ideology. To criticize ideology requires, therefore, the criticism of utopian thinking.

The essay of M. Darrol Bryant in this volume is an instructive introduction to the dialectical relation between utopian thinking and Christian eschatology. Bryant uses the struggles of Jonathan Edwards, America's greatest theologian, as a case study. Bryant argues that Edwards used three levels of criticism: (1) utopian thinking used as a principle of social criticism; (2) apocalyptic thinking used as a principle of criticism of utopian thinking; (3) trinitarian thinking used as a principle of criticism of apocalyptic thinking. In this way, Bryant shows us how Edwards struggled to distinguish between man's vision of an historical fulfillment and man's vision of a fulfillment beyond history.

The concrete implication of the distinction between utopian thinking and eschatology is the maintenance of the conditions of criticism itself. This includes, too, the maintenance of a distinction between the Church as eschatological reality and the Church as now existing "between the ages." The essay by Johann Baptist

Metz deals with this question. Metz argues that the Church is neither the religious expression of society as a whole nor is it a utopian movement against society. The classical sociological distinction between "church" and "sect" described the religious movements of a society as either accommodating or revolutionary. Metz argues that the true Church must be plural; it must be both. It is itself a *tension*, a compromise, a maintenance of diversity that seeks to balance and hold together incompatible (at least in any given moment) values and demands. The Church in this world is a political reality. In this way, Metz, like Bryant and Moltmann, engages in an attempt to disentangle Christian eschatology from utopian thinking, and to determine critically the proper sphere and function of each.

JÜRGEN MOLTMANN

1. The Cross and Civil Religion

Translated by Thomas Hughson and Paul Rigby
Introduction by Thomas Hughson

Introduction

In "The Cross and Civil Religion," Jürgen Moltmann critically revises his theology of hope while also developing its implications. His essay deserves its title on two counts: its fundamental perspective is theological; its aim is a critical evaluation of frequently overlooked political realities. The most important of these is "civil religion." "Civil religion" designates religion as it functions politically—an aspect frequently unrecognized by religions themselves. This aspect has been located through the analysis worked out by Feuerbach, Marx, and Freud, who continued the critical method of the German Enlightenment. Their analysis is "functional" because it asks of a concrete religion (which is always within a political community) what are its social, economic, and psychic functions within the life of its believers and their society? In doing this, a functional analysis ignores the content of the doctrines and the explicit professions of faith.

Moltmann seeks to use this functional method as the foundation for his theological critique. For such a critique to be "theological," more is required than that it be undertaken by a theologian; it must also be employed theologically. Traditionally, theological doctrines such as eschatology have not been given a functional analysis. To use the method successfully is no little achievement, for it is to coordinate within a single viewpoint both some of the German Enlightenment's important insights and traditional theology's own insights, without sacrificing one to the other. Thus, the final question to be asked of Moltmann's essay will not be "what did he do?" but "has he succeeded?" If that much has been clarified, the North American reader can put what is perhaps the most interesting question: How does Moltmann's line of theological reflection instruct our own styles of thought? Moltmann's enterprise can be assessed most profitably in its reinterpretation of the theology of Christ's crucifixion.

Moltmann prefaces his essay with the remark that he intends to extend his theology of hope into politics with the help of the theology of the cross. Moltmann's theology of the cross draws upon both the theology of Luther and the method of functional analysis. Accordingly, the question becomes, How can the cross of Christ function within the political community? Many have accused the cross of enshrining resignation, indifference to history, or surrender to circumstances. Such views of the cross could never found a theology of hope or a political theology. By employing the "functional method" to understand the cross, Moltmann locates a political factor in the forces crucifying Christ, since Christ was officially executed by the Roman Empire. Further, this was no accident of history, for in Moltmann's view, Christ's eschatological message attacked every state's claim to absolute loyalty. Functionally, Christ was seditious. Functionally, his crucifixion was a regnant government's repression of an alternative ultimate value that would relativize its own claims to be absolute. Functionally, the cross was the initial rejection by the Church of all political structures seeking to become religions. In this sense, the cross represents divine rejection of political and civil religion.

We can understand Moltmann's aim more clearly if we consider the historical context out of which he writes. In its broadest perspective, Moltmann's essay continues the Enlightenment's critique of civil religions. More immediately, Moltmann writes against the efforts of modern nation-states to develop patriotic civil religions. He sees this tendency present in America today just as it was in Germany a generation ago. For Moltmann, the experience of Hitler and the Third Reich is the decisive, living context out of which he writes.

Moltmann wishes to dissociate himself from the German lawyer and political theorist Carl Schmitt, whose doctrine was used as the ideological justification of Hitler's National Socialist party. Not surprisingly, Moltmann also wishes to connect up with the political tradition of Karl Barth and the Confessing Church which opposed Hitler. Carl Schmitt's political theory gave the ideological justification for Hitler's National Socialist party, by allowing it to pose as the restorer of authority and social justice. Following Hobbes, Schmitt believed that the state alone could guarantee such justice, for it alone could protect its citizens from internal and external enemies. The state had to be sufficient to ensure this law and order in human affairs, and it alone had this responsibility. (This is what Moltmann means when he says that Schmitt held that "politics is everything.") However, Schmitt believed that the parliamentary system of the Weimar Republic was inadequate to ensure justice in twentieth-century mass society. Therefore, Schmitt's doctrine could be used as an ideological justification for a Germany guided by principles of leadership and loyalty. It dovetailed with Schmitt's doctrine that any legal order is based on sovereign decisions grounded not in positive norms but in emergency decrees. Schmitt called this "decisionism."

Hitler's aim was to assimilate the German Evangelical Church to the national-socialist state. In 1933, church elections were held under the auspices of the "Deutsche Christen," which was the national-socialist organization of the church. So decisive was the majority which Hitler won in this election that opposition to him arose and culminated in 1934 in the first Confessional synod of Barmen. Karl Barth spearheaded the opposition with his *Theological Existence Today*. The synod's "Barmen Declaration" rejected Nazism so effectively that Hitler abandoned his attempt to create one state church. Instead, he restrained the church's independence by financial control. In response, the Christian opposition organized itself independently as the Confessing Church. Unfortunately, in 1935, the Confessing Church was itself split internally by theological disputes and conflicting attitudes towards Nazism. It underestimated the Nazis and, instead of total opposition, attempted to gain state recognition. Slowly, it was rendered ineffective, and was persecuted and almost phased out during the war. In 1945, the Confessing Church reassembled as the Evangelical Church. But it had learned its lesson: it rejected the last remnants of state control. This independence and the critical distance which it gives has become the essence of Moltmann's political theology.

The Cross and Civil Religion

Every eschatological theology must become socially critical if it is to become a political theology.
                                                    Johann Baptist Metz

I would like to move in the above direction by applying my "theology of hope"—with a theological principle of antithesis—to the whole area of political life. The theology of the cross is the principle of antithesis that makes this step possible. Moreover, to emphasize the theology of the cross in this way shows it to be an inevitable consequence flowing from the theory and practice of the theology of hope.

I. What is Contemporary Political Theology? What should it be?

Words too have their destiny. They are not as ineffectual as one sometimes thinks. They can serve as stage cues. Often, they do more than call an actor to the stage: if the script of the play is not yet written, cues evoke confusion and discussion. Or else they may stir up a hornet's nest, unleash the devil and trigger defense mechanisms.

J. B. Metz's recent challenging call for a political theology has worked as such a cue. The older actors remember an older play and react in shock. Spectres appear before them—political Catholicism, Prussian court preachers, and German Christian heresies. They pull down from the shelf Carl Schmitt's *Political Theology* (1922, 1934), look up dictionary articles, and find the term suspect. They regard it as just one more case of theologians meddling in politics. On the other hand, younger actors have different recollections and associate better hopes with the cue. They read the past in the mirror of Rolf Hochhuth's *The Deputy*, Dietrich Bonhoeffer's *The Cost of Discipleship* and perhaps even

14

the 1945 Stuttgart acknowledgment of guilt made by the Confessing Church. By contrast, the younger actors experience a contemporary Church of the neutral middle with its conciliatory policy of no politics. Amazed, they ask how, after Auschwitz and Hiroshima, one can believe in any kind of relation between the Church and the state. For them, too, the idea of a "political theology" evokes the Age of Constantine and an antiquated idea of what theology's task is.

However, the feelings stirred up by political theology cannot be analyzed at this level. They lie still deeper, in repressed guilt and rationalized omissions. Generally, we are anesthetized to internal theological disputes. But political theology somehow gets on our nerves. Politics in this age is democratic; Protestantism is restless. The Christian citizenry oscillates between the "confessions of an apolitical German" (Thomas Mann) and the sudden reversals that shout "Politics is everything!" (Carl Schmitt).

The problems and repressions that the cue "political theology" prompts have resulted, since 1945, in a series of bold initiatives in Evangelical theology. The genus of political homily developed within the sphere of influence of Karl Barth's theology. Already in 1934, Barth said:

> It (namely the Confessing Church) has to some extent struggled seriously for the freedom and purity of its kerygma; however, it has remained silent about, for example, steps taken against the Jews, the astonishing treatment of the political opposition, the suppression of truth in the press of modern Germany and much else to which the Old Testament prophets would have addressed themselves with assurance.

In 1946, Barth declared:

> It is not a good sign if the community is in fear and trembling when a homily becomes political: as if it could be apolitical. . . . The community that is aware of its political responsibility will want and demand that a homily become political; the community will understand it politically even if the word "political" remains unspoken.

In 1952, he exclaimed:

> What kind of a kerygma is it which, out of single-minded preoccupation with the illicit advent of the eschaton, has nothing better to

offer to man living, erring and suffering in 1952 but a tired "reference to the ambiguity and transitoriness of all political acts!"

Reactionary sermons in the past criticized Karl Barth in the same way as reactionary sermons today protest the Cologne "Political Evening Prayer." These sermons said "yes" to homilies which left their political consequences to the individual to draw out, but "no" to political homilies. They said "yes" to worship with possible political consequences, but "no" to a political church. They said "yes" to Christians politically come of age, but "no" to a political church. Politics, they said, may be the private and accidental result of the work of the church, but it should not be permitted to become the criterion of eligibility. According to them, even in a democratic society, churches should claim no political mandate (a pre-democratic idea!). It is evidently the opinion that the Church can be an institution of reconciliation only if it remains impartial and nonpartisan, squarely in the socio-political middle. Here it can remain innocuous; it caters to and is patronized by all sides. However, the Church can perform this role only at the price of binding itself in institutionalized neutrality.

More recently, Romans 13 has been exegetically demythologized and the traditional appeal to this text systematically explained away. In the realm of political ethics the scarcely Christianized metaphysic of authority has been replaced by a new "political morality" (E. Wolff). The belief in the single "kingship of Christ" has prevailed over the "German ideology" that affirmed the separation of spiritual and temporal realms. There has been a stress on the daily service of God in the realm of routine work (E. Käsemann) and the obligation to political obedience (H. Gollwitzer). The characteristics of these analyses are practical politics and socioethical directives on the right to dissent, on democratic constitution, on rearmament, on conscientious objection, on the recognition of the Oder-Neisse line, etc.

Nevertheless, the two approaches ("ecclesial neutrality" or "political morality") have not sufficiently analyzed the relation of *logos* to *ethos*, or of theory to practice. In the present Church, the role of political homilies and directives has remained radically unexplicated, with the result that the critique of ideologies and institutions goes unnoticed. The model for shaping and publishing the Church's political directives has remained nonbinding and arbitrary, since the Church has wished to treat problems pragmatically. But we should ask: can we do better than that?

There are resources available to the Church for a comprehensive approach to politics. An initial resource is the historical-critical method of modern biblical exegesis. This has examined the history of its texts from political and sociological viewpoints, but has scarcely ever examined itself and the present forms of the Church in society. K. Koch states: "In form-history, literary criticism and sociology are contiguous since each literary form expresses a 'sociological fact.' This knowledge prevents an all too simple distinction between intellectual history and economic-political history." Despite this, the results of form-historical analysis have been interpreted existentially, without attention to the form-historical or sociological function of existential interpretations in modern society (e.g., Bultmann). An interpretation of the Bible oriented solely to intellectual history reveals the historicity of the individual, but thereby unconsciously dehistoricizes the social structures in which he lives. It does not go beyond the idealistic conception of person. It even neglects the idealistic insight into the dialectic of person and external relations, as well as their reciprocal transformations. Form-historical method should have opened up the way long ago for the transition from the historical study of the Church's past to the sociopolitical study of its present reality. Have present theology, church, homilies, essays, pamphlets, been subjected to form-history, i.e. to a sociopolitical interpretation? What relevant language can be used in the contemporary social crisis? We can only be consistent if we pass from a historical to a sociocritical and political viewpoint. Not only will texts then be clearly understood, but there will also be critical reflection on their actual sociopolitical origins in a world divided by dichotomies—private and public, spiritual and political, inner and outer.

A second resource for approaching politics is the critique of religion offered by the German Enlightenment. Feuerbach, Marx, Freud and their successors do not ask about "true religion" (as in earlier religious debates), but about the psychic, social, and political functions of religion and church. Today, the destiny of man is, as they saw, less and less dependent on natural environment and more and more dependent on technical civilization, urbanization, social milieu, and politics. Accordingly, a theological critique must take into account the social-psychological and political functions of homilies, of religious institutions, religious ideas and the behavior patterns of the believer in the net of interaction and interdependence in modern life.

Theology that wants to be responsible today must consider self-critically the psychological and political implications of its words, images, and symbols. It can no longer view the Church's institutional tasks as merely given and neutral, thereby opting out in indifference. It must scrutinize each discourse about God: Does the Church supply people with religious opium or a real ferment of freedom? This does not mean, as many say, that theology should cease to speak of God in order to attend to the class struggle or the progress of mankind. It means, rather, that theology must analyze its every word to see whether it is speaking of the God of the crucified Christ rather than of the Baal of the nations and the idols of the heart. It must examine itself to see whether it disseminates faith or superstition. Implied, moreover, is that theology must be self-critical concerning the efficacy of the Church's institutions. We should pose not only this question: What is the linguistic meaning of our speaking about God, but further ask what public effect it has in a given situation to speak of God (or to remain silent).

Effects are difficult to forecast with accuracy; the future is usually surprising. The relations between assertion and action, word and deed, hearing and effect, are obscure and require explication. There are many unknowns and human reactions are inconsistent. Responsible ethics must test Christian intentions and actions by their results and responses—which never fully correspond. The character of this interdependence must be considered. Particularly problematic are institutions where this interdependence is intricate and convoluted. Critical reflection on church institutions must examine and raise to consciousness that which has been taken for granted.

Political theology, in our opinion, no longer implies only theology and politics, church and state. Rather, responsible theology must become aware of an inherent political dimension in itself and in church life. On the other hand, political theology does not reduce everything to politics (C. Schmitt) nor does it submit theology and the Church to the terms and requirements of state policy. Nor does it aim to make political questions the central themes of Christian theology. (This would be analogous to supposing that theology of the "cross" makes the cross the exclusive source of Christian knowledge of God.) Political theology denotes rather the field, the milieu, the realm, and the stage on which Christian theology should be explicitly carried on today. Political theology wants to awaken political consciousness in every treatise of Christian theology. Understood in this way, it is the premise that leads to the conclusion that, while there may be naive and politically unaware theology, there can be no apolitical theology. Overtly "apolitical theology" is frequently covertly allied with political movements that are, for the most part, conservative. Churches, therefore, that retire into an apolitical neutrality which they believe puts them above politics are nonetheless politically involved. However, their privileged position and exemption from politics costs them their critical leadership. The real question is not whether the churches should be allowed to become political, as critics keep on fearing, but whether the Church can extricate itself from the unconscious, hidden compromising practice of political theology. The Church must develop a critical and self-conscious political theology.

We conceive political theology, therefore, as the new perspective for all Christian theology. This new method, or fundamental category, cannot ignore the fact that its own interests are also shared by political religions and political theologies that reduce religion and theology to politics. Critics of the left and the right have justly objected that this new political theology, without some theological principle of antithesis, is the old enterprise in a new guise. They rightly fear that a political theology will justify the status quo and prevailing ideologies. We must immediately agree that "the affinity of the eschatological message of Jesus to the social-political reality" (Metz) implies a critical theology. But this "eschatological proviso" is no adequate foundation for a critique of this society. The eschatological admonition with its reference to the "not yet" underscores the provisional nature of every historically evolved society. This prevents the immediate identification and direct politicizing of Christian promises in any historical situation. H. Maier sees only one difference between the new and the old political theologies. The new places these identifications and politicizings of Christ's promise in the future, while the old places them in the past or the present. In Maier's judgment, the eschatological proviso has become a "not yet" within history. But Maier overlooks the distinction between the Christian message and modern ideology. If the eschatological proviso and the Pauline "not yet" are merely the negative pole for a positive "but then," the difference between eschatology and ideology is only quantitative and temporal. In this case, present social, critical, and political theology would be but a forerunner of the political theology that would universally prevail in a world utopia.

The old theology of natural order could be understood as sanctioning the social status quo. If today's critic opposes to this only a theology of change, then this new theology is only the sanctioning of a new society founded upon rapid change. If theology today is to become socially critical, it must stop short of underwriting that social critique which is admittedly indispensable to any modern society. Sociocritical theology can only mean the confrontation of the Church and believers with their own deepest profession. Critical theology springs from the source and center of the Church. Without a critical theology, the Church ends up accommodating itself to present structure, change, and critique.

The specifically Christian quality and critique expressed in the eschatological proviso is not quantitative and temporal, but qualitative and trans-temporal. Christian theology may not lag behind Herbert Marcuse's insight that it is important for critical theory to focus on "the scandal of the qualitative difference" in the revolutionary deed itself, "if critical theory does not wish to stop at merely improving the existing state of affairs."[1] For my part, I want to remind the reader that I identify the Pauline theology of hope with his theology of the cross and have spoken of an "eschatology of the cross." Against Corinthian Christianity, with its realized eschatology, Paul issued his antiutopian "not yet" as the complement of the words that he had preached to them about the cross.

Metz, too, places the theological-political event of the crucifixion of Christ, who is the bearer of eschatological promises, at the center of critical political theology. In this way he moves beyond the old type of critique that seeks to show the provisional nature of the supposedly definitive present. That which at once mediates and differentiates the kingdom of God and the world, the eschatological future and political history, must not be turned into a metaphysics. For to separate the transitory from the permanent, the penultimate from the ultimate, what is of man from what is of God, it is enough to gaze upon the cross of Christ which separates as well as binds. What God has joined together in Christ let no man put asunder in metaphysics. The "scandal of the qualitative difference" lies not in the otherworldliness of Christian hope but in the sign of the cross present in this world. It is exactly here that Christian theology, to become politically critical, must part from the "political theology" that led to the crucifixion of Jesus. Only if this difference is made clearer can the accusation be warded off that a so-called critical awareness has been installed for ideological reasons. For the danger is that this critical awareness be taken as merely a sophisticated version of the prevailing uncritical and instinctual religious mentality whose motivation and function remain unexamined. We will, therefore, begin with an analysis of "political religion" as expressed in political metaphysics. This will lead, in section five, to an investigation of the political implications of a theology of the cross.

II. Political Religion

Political religions, as formulated in political theologies, are not the invention of Christianity, for ancient pagan religions are essentially political. Christian faith and theology have their origin in the political crucifixion of Christ and have fought the political religions of peoples and states. This subject has been sufficiently dealt with in the history of ideas by E. Peterson, A. Ehrhardt, H. Maier, and E. Feil. A few recollections and observations drawn from this history will be sufficient to introduce the contemporary scene.

The expressions "political theology," *theologia civilis*, *genus politikon* come from Stoic philosophy. Panaitos distinguishes three classes of divinities: personified powers of nature, the gods of the state religion, and those in myths (i.e., physical, political, mythical divinities). He builds on this the tripartite theology that was particularly successful within the rationalism of ancient Roman theology. In Terrentius Varro, this scheme finds its first literary expression. Augustine discusses his opinion in the *City of God*, book 6, chapter 12: the poets fashion images of the gods in myth, the philosophers in theological reflections on nature and metaphysics, the community in politics. Mythical theology is particularly suited to the theater (the cultic-political theater). Metaphysical theology belongs to the philosophical schools. Political theology is used by the state. Augustine discerns a split between mythical and political theology on the one hand and metaphysical theology on the other. The former two, which are simultaneously mythic and political, belong to theater, temple, and public entertainments of a particular community. The latter (i.e., the purely intellectual, abstract cult of philosophical religion) is universal; hence it tends toward a cosmic religion unifying the whole of mankind. The Greek stoa esteemed above all the theology of nature. The Roman stoa preferred an incipient political theology, for as Varro said, "What the poets wrote is too common to serve as a model for the people. What the philosophers think is too sublime to be helpful for the people." Therefore, the poets and the philosophers are supposed to promote a civil theology. For in a political community, both citizens and priests must know somehow which gods are recognized by the state and which services and sacrifices have official sanction.

Ancient political theory joined together state and gods. There were no godless states, no stateless gods. City and community, *polis* and *civitas*, law and justice, *nomos* and *dike* were religious ideas. Ancient social doctrine holds knowledge and worship of the gods of the fatherland to be of the utmost importance in securing prosperity and peace for the nation. To this end citizens united in a common religion. By the Hellenistic period, this organizational principle, the polis, became itself the object of religious worship. Both the divinization of the polis and the creation of the goddess Roma were influenced by the East. This is not unheard of today: Indian national independence created a new goddess, Mother India.

Roman political theology is the source of the ancient and enduring trilogy: religion, authority, and tradition (Hannah Arendt). Nevertheless, it is noteworthy that public religious cult alone was an obligatory civic duty, while there was liberty in private and domestic religion. This is clear from the laws governing religious crimes. "The theoretical repudiation of state religion . . . is not sufficient grounds for the charge of *crimen laesae religionis* ("crime against religion"); one became indictable only for neglecting the public obligation of religious cult." (Cyprian Martyr: *Imperatores praeceperunt eos qui Romanam religionem non colunt debere Romanas caeremonias recognoscere.* It was therefore, completely irrelevant whether one refused to worship the gods of the state because one was atheist or whether one refused to worship them because one worshipped other Gods. Atheism meant only one thing: public refusal to participate in the civic cult, cultic impiety against the gods of the state. Christians were first accused of atheism in this context. Justin Martyr says he called himself an atheist for precisely this offense against the Roman gods (Apol. I, 6, 13). Later, the laws of the Christian emperors Theodosius and Justinian raised Christianity into a state religion resembling the religion of earlier Rome. From then on, Jewish synagogues were considered sacrilegious and all non-Christian religions were regarded as species of atheism. Positive and negative laws guiding political theism demonstrate the presence of Christian "political religion" at the time of Constantine. Through the Christianization of Europe, Christianity became heir to the traditional and official Roman state religion. Christianity became a political religion in the sense that its religiosity expressed a political raison d'etre.

We must now ask whether the substance of political religion has disappeared from modern, pluralistic, laicized and partially emancipated societies. A survey of legislation on blasphemy, past and present, throughout Europe, from Spain to the U.S.S.R., shows a transition from gods protected by the state to gods who are patrons of religious groupings in states indifferent to religion. This legislation has as its counterpart legislation to protect state symbols against defamation, which shows that the location of political religion has merely shifted. Even where, as in the United States, there is separation of church and state, there can arise an indigenous civil religion. Similarly, the German constitution was composed, as the preamble says, "in the awareness of its responsibility before God and man" (though which "God" remains an open question). This "God" has been invoked by both Protestant and Catholics in their church services. If we go deeper, religious psychology shows clearly the "instinctual religious mentality" that clings with religious ardor to political father-figures to gain solace and security. This mentality defends itself against the threat of public atheism by affirming that atheism is an intellectual rootlessness that undermines custom and the state. When, on the other hand, socialistic church policy subordinates the Church to reasons of state, then this is nothing but atheistic church policy. It is yet another political religion, except that here the state religion is a state ideology. Even the separation of church and state does not impede the formation and practice of political religion. As in former times, political religion today provides the symbolic integration and mythical self-ratification of a society.

III. *The First Christian Critique of Political Religion*

Early Christians were known and punished as godless and seditious followers of Christ, who had been similarly punished as an insurgent by the same pagan philosophers and Roman senate. We should never forget this early Christian conflict with state religion, even though Christian apologists tried to explain from the start the Christian faith as the authentic support of the state and to expound Christian theology as the fulfillment of political theology.

E. Peterson, in his celebrated treatise on "Monotheism as a Political Problem" (1935), arguing against Carl Schmitt's "Political Theology," delineated the political aspect in the history of Christian dogma. Christian philosophy early tried to combine biblical monotheism with the philosophical monotheism of the Aristotelian school. This metaphysical monotheism is basically monarchical: just as there is only one God, so he has only one world rule. The universe too has a monarchical structure: one God, one *logos* and *nomos*, one cosmos. God, by being identified with the unity of reality, becomes the symbol producing this unity. This monotheistic world view in natural theology corresponds in political theology to the dominion of an emperor. Aristotle himself recognized the convertibility of these metaphysical and political ideas. The familiar text with which he concludes the twelfth book of his metaphysics crowns his metaphysical theology: "Things do not wish to be misgoverned. Multiple sovereignty is not good. Let there be one sovereign." These words of Aristotle come from the *Iliad*, where Agamemnon speaks them with political intent. Carl Schmitt traced this notion of unity in the history of theism, deism, and naturalism and their corresponding constitutional forms. By so doing, Schmitt was able to present his doctrine of "decisionism" in which he taught that the emergency decrees of a ruler constitute the preliminary form of a metaphysics of unity. Christian apologists adopted this methodological structure of convertibility: they turned the early Christian polemic against the tolerant polytheistic Roman religion into the Christian theological foundation of the future Roman empire. They rejected the political theology of the people, but politicized the natural theology of the philosophers, and in this way won over the educated classes who were among the despisers of political religion. Polytheism was, in effect, replaced by the one Church assembling the many peoples and their religions under the one God. The notion of one God and the belief in one universal Church called for a corresponding political policy. Hence, Peterson concludes, "To the one earthly king corresponded the one God, the one heavenly King who ruled with one royal Law and Logos."

The parallel between the peaceful reign of Christ and the Pax Romana was demonstrated by the simultaneous birth of Christ the Savior and the accession of Augustus to imperial power. When Christ's reign of peace and the Pax Romana were believed to have been joined by God's providence, Christianity had to surrender its separate existence. For as soon as this political and religious peace enveloped the inhabited world, then Christianity became the religion unifying these kingdoms. The post-Constantinian struggle between church and emperor was likewise the struggle for the liberation of Christian theology from this political theology of Rome.

Peterson has further shown how political-religious monotheism was overcome by the formation of the doctrine of the Trinity. The mystery of three persons is in God, not in creation. The Christian doctrine of the Trinity rewrites the unity of God the Father to include the crucified Christ in the Holy Spirit. If the revelation of God in the crucified Christ is the primary datum, then the Christian God can no longer be used as the religious scaffolding for sovereignties, authorities, and powers. Peterson, unfortunately, was not bold enough to point out that the trinitarian doctrine also serves as a critique of the hierarchical Church's monarchical episcopate. This kind of episcopate corresponded exactly to Roman political monotheism and adopted the titles, honors, and court ceremonial of the fallen Roman empire. The doctrine of the Trinity liberated Christian theology from religiopolitical monotheism, which it destroyed in principle if not in fact. The political function of the doctrine of the Trinity is, I think, even today to criticize political religion. Christianity is not "radically monotheistic" (H. Richard Niebuhr). Christianity is trinitarian.

Traditionally, the dogmatic treatise "de Deo" was divided into a natural theology that speaks of God's unity and a theology of revelation that unfolds the mystery of the three persons. This clearly reflects the traditional engrafting of revealed Christian faith (Trinity) onto the natural political religion of a nation (God's unity). The liberal rejection of trinitarian doctrine was the signal for the dissolving of the Christian faith into a political religion for "the Christian world." Therefore, Karl Barth consciously began his church dogmatics with the doctrine of the Trinity without a prolegomena on natural theology. This is not the Church withdrawing from the world of politics but the Church offering a radical critique of any political theology. This can be seen if one reads Barth's *Church Dogmatics* in the context of his earlier dialectical writings.

The synthesis of the Pax Christi with the Pax Romana shattered, according to Peterson, Christian eschatology. The peace of God which passes all understanding—political understanding included— issues not from any Caesar, but from the crucified Christ alone. Yet does this peace only surpass all understanding, or is it rather a scandal and a folly to modern knowledge? The Christian gains critical distance from technocratic and revolutionary ideals of peace not from gazing upon heavenly promises, but in confronting the kingdom of God on the cross.

Peterson sees that Christian trinitarian doctrine and eschatology completed the break between Christian theology and every political theology that justifies the political status quo. H. Maier and R. Spaemann think nothing further is necessary except to recognize the ongoing necessity of this break. But it seems to me that the political problematic of Christian theology begins here. For if the Church, as Maier recommends, holds itself "above all political understanding," then it does not threaten this political theology. Only if the "either Christ or Caesar" antinomy is allowed to flare up can there be dialectical and productive tensions.

IV. *Postdenominational "Political Theology"*

1. After the medieval dispute between the emperor and the pope, the ancient idea of a unified religious and political community was resurrected in the Renaissance humanism of Europe. In the nationalizing church movements, the ancient regal symbols were displaced by the new nationalist symbols of the "people"—on the model of the tribal federation under Moses. In the Protestant national churches, the medieval conception of a *corpus Christianum* was revived on the smaller scale of national powers. Machiavellian religious politics was eagerly adopted; religion assisted greatly in keeping the army in obedience, the nation in unity, and the populace in contentment. Hobbes recommended the ancient advice: "The state has the absolute right to command which names and titles of God should be socially binding and which not" (*De Civitate* 15). Even today religious sociology must consult Rousseau's *The Social Contract*, book 4, chapter 8, for his masterful analysis of the structures of "civil religion." According to Rousseau, Jesus founded on earth a spiritual kingdom based on the separation of theological from political systems, thereby separating religious from civil institutions. The result was a "religion of man" and a "religion of citizens." The former consisted in inner veneration of the supreme God and in pure and simple gospel religion, or in authentic belief in God and in divine natural law. The latter was restricted to a particular country and its own divinities and protective patrons and constituted civil religion or divine positive law. Thus reverence was given to the fatherland and at the same time to the protective divinity. According to Rousseau, the "religion of man," or Chris-

tianity, restricted the power of civil law. Rousseau, all too opti-
mistically, said, "I know nothing which restrains nationalism more
than Christianity, for the gospel establishes no national religion and
it is therefore impossible to have a holy war among Christians."
However, even positive civil religions have their dogmas. These
must be few in number and self-evident. Rousseau listed four
dogmas: (1) the existence of the Almighty; (2) an all-encompas-
sing Providence; (3) an afterlife; (4) reward for the good and
punishment for the wicked. Robert Bellah has shown that civil
religion in America can likewise be reduced to these four points.
A poll has demonstrated that the same four points characterize
German belief: omnipotence, providence, life after death, and just
judgment—all concepts which the state can use to its advantage.

2. In modern times there has been a further development of
"political theology." Augustine associated mythical with political
theology. These two, expressed as cultic tradition and state myth,
together opposed any natural theology. Before Augustine, the
Christian apologists had not dealt with individual political theologies, but rather had politicized the universal natural theology
into a Catholic theology. In modern times, Christian denominations
have become the actual political religions of independent nation-
states. As this occurred, the idea of a "natural religion" and a
"natural theology" arose within humanism. This idea of a natural
religion was used to oppose the political religions of warring nation-
states. In sum, one can understand modern "natural theology" as
the antithesis of political theologies. The controversy between Karl
Barth and Emil Brunner in the dark years around 1933 over "nature
and grace" was misleading. They never posed questions of "natural
theology" or "revelation theology," but considered only *Deutsche
Christen* theology, which was merely a religious rationalization for
the Third Reich.

Modern natural theology drew its sustenance from Stoic humanism but had its own tragic irony. It understood itself as the launching
of a postdenominational and post-Christian era. This natural theology involved a radical inversion of the relation between reason
and revelation, nature and grace, state and church. Hence, G.
Söhngen writes: "Before the Enlightenment, natural theology was
only a preparation for divine wisdom and doctrine. But in modern

times, all supernatural and suprarational elements of religion became mere prolegomena; religion now constituted the horizon for natural theology. In modern times, the supernatural and supranatural elements of religion became merely the historically given. These became the data for constructing ethical rationalism." At the Enlightenment, Lessing reversed Protestant orthodoxy's "reason and revelation" to "revelation and reason." Natural, rational knowledge of God, once a study of the history of man's sin and God's revelation, was now transformed into a study of the goal of history. Natural theology was no longer the description and analysis of secular history into which revelation entered; it became the eschatological goal of history which historical revelation promised. Thus the revised natural theology intended to continue the task of earlier religious revelation and faith. Lessing's and Kant's religious understanding of history reveal the modern philosophical millenarianism of "natural theology." The theme of earlier natural theology had been that the existence of God the Creator could be shown with certainty by reason from the evidence of creation. This was changed into a new theme: the hope that in the future, God would be "all in all" to pure human reason and that "no one will have to instruct another" for "each would be immediately aware of God." "Enlightenment" was the transition from particular Church beliefs to universal belief in reason. Kant's religious utopia of a purely rational religion saw itself as a powerful critique in the service of this transition. This corresponded to his utopia of a just cosmopolis and its critical power against the world of nation-states.

Natural theology was made the starting point of a cosmopolitan critique of religion. Such a cosmopolitan critique can only be considered as the negation of many civil religions and denominations. Basically the critique politicized what Rousseau called "the religion of man" in order to overcome the state religions. The French and American humanists were political humanists. They advocated the "religion of man" and the "natural rights of man" as public reality. They spoke not simply of freedom, or freedom of choice and thought, but of "public freedom." They demanded not simply the right to individual happiness but to "public happiness." Thomas Jefferson declared, "No one can be called happy without his participation in public happiness. No one can be called free unless he experiences public freedom. No one can be called happy or free unless he shares in and contributes to public power." The politicizing of modern natural theology had two tendencies. First, it oriented itself toward the universality of a future religion of man. It worked critically for the dissolution of national religions and the passing of the confessional period of Christianity. Second it sought to democratize public life and to overcome the separation of public and private. We find both tendencies in Richard Rothe, the father of the modern theories of secularization. For him, the modern Christian spirit relinquished its "ecclesial phase" to enter its "political phase."

It is helpful to distinguish between (a) political theologies that articulate an actual "civil religion," (b) pre-Christian natural theologies that are quite distinct from the political theologies (or theologies of the *polis*) in ancient times, and (c) postdenominational modern natural theologies that inherit their millennarian bias from Christian eschatology. The political implications of modern natural theology must not be confused with the civil religion mentioned above.

3. In Germany, several different parties in election campaigns take their turn in playing upon the feelings peculiar to civil religion. They offer nonpartisan father-figures and national myths of protection and security, paying tribute to what Paul Tillich called in 1933 "political romanticism." They claim the golden mean between the devilish snares of the right and the left and caricature their opponents. Axel Springer (the major German publisher of popular magazines and newspapers) has most clearly recognized the religio-political needs of authoritarian people and built his publishing house by catering to these needs. In their everyday gnosticism, they see the world as black and white. Good proves the existence of God, and bad, that of the devil. Journalistic "pastoral care" must not show only the bad; it must report and promote the good. But the good must be shown to be so ambiguous that no one will think he can promote it by joining a radical political party. All radicals must be silenced by showing the world's ambivalence and their own paradoxical situation. Even when this pastoral theology is inadequate, "eccentric minorities" are not to be allowed a voice. Should political questions become more important to the Church than

questions of belief, then "out of a sense of Christian responsibility" the press steps in to guide men to this belief. Hence, says Springer, "All else that we as the press can muster—news, persuasion, entertainment—are the resources for this great task." Should the Church become politically critical, it would leave a vacuum in the soul of the people which other "pastors" must fill. Hence, Springer! His publishing network seizes upon the opportunity that falls into its lap. He seeks to provide pastoral care for those whom he describes as "respectable Christians."

If Church and theology play the role of political critic, then they should be wary of superficial slogans about the true situation; neither should they be caught up by "secular," "liberated," and "pluralistic" society. Instead, they should work for the liberation of men and women from the merely "instinctual religious mentality" that yearns for a Springer journalistic ministry, father-myths, and security. This critical political task requires courage to violate our "holiest feelings" and courage to bear the sanctions of society.

4. Recently in the United States, the sociologist of religion, Robert Bellah, published his celebrated article "Civil Religion in America."[2] Bellah showed, from the inaugural speeches of American presidents, that there is a civil religion in the United States, a religion that upholds the separation of church and state. This civil religion has its own dignity and its own rites. In the pilgrim fathers, it is "messianic" (Exodus and chosen people); in its social critique and Revolution, "prophetic;" and in Abraham Lincoln and the civil war, "martyred"—life out of death: "The dead have died so that the nation might live." Though American civil religion has worship, holidays, and symbols, it cannot be identified with Protestantism, Catholicism, or Judaism. It inspires and mobilizes the people, as in Roosevelt's New Deal, Kennedy's New Frontier, and the civil rights movement. It can, however, be used merely for national self-justification and arrogance, e.g., the planting of the American instead of the United Nations flag on the moon. (This act was, however, opposed by many Americans.) Bellah's critique of civil religion uses a distinction between particular and universal: "As Americans, we have been well-favored in the world, but it is as men that we will be judged." Bellah sees that the messianic and prophetic symbols of American civil religion can be misused for

imperialistic ends. Still, according to its best intentions, "a world civil religion" can be seen as the fulfillment rather than as the destruction of the American dream. "Indeed, such an outcome has been the eschatological hope of American civil religion from the beginning."

Because American theologians usually think of "natural theology" as a prolegomenon to the teachings of the church, they have failed to understand its potential danger as the teaching of a "civil religion." Hence, Karl Barth's vigorous "No" to natural theology is frequently misunderstood by American theologians, and Barth's *Church Dogmatics* strikes them as clerical. It is significant, however, that the theologians of the "other America" understand Barth's theology as a critical and political theology of the cross. They feel themselves excluded from that white civil religion; and so they have little interest in "natural theology."[3]

As early as 1961, P. Berger in *The Noise of Solemn Assemblies: Christian Commitment and the Religious Establishment in America*[4] had similarly described this civil religion, though at that time his neoorthodox viewpoint led him to see the disestablishment of the civil religion as the Christian task. "The God of Moses, who refused to give His name for magical use, is the same God who comes to us in Jesus Christ. And it may even be relevant to remind our religious mental hygienists that Jesus of Nazareth was crucified. We suspect that it is a theological task in our situation to elaborate the eschatological character of the Christian faith against the this-worldliness of American religiosity, to set justification by faith against our pervasive legalism, to explain the meaning of the cross in a culture that glorifies success and happiness." That is not just an intellectual task for theologians, for: "This rejection of religion is an important element of what we may call 'the other America,' that America which is denied and repressed in the 'community of the respectable.' "

Bellah sees the relative justification of American civil religion in its ambitious horizon of bringing about a world religion; Berger sets in the forefront the Christian task of disestablishing this civil religion by means of a theology of the cross. Bellah's proposal can be a relative justification of the status quo in the name of the future; Berger's, however, can also be used as a justification for the status quo, since he turns to the "Wholly Other" or a Christian "great refusal." This is why it is theologically important to conceive eschatology and the theology of the cross as one. This is why it is practically important to join together the hope of a universal society with the actual struggle of people who are oppressed and neglected. In this way, Christian churches serve neither as the religion nor as the sects of society.

It is not enough to make Christian theology relevant at the expense of the prophetic-apostolic tradition or of the universalism of God's kingdom and law. Nor will it do merely to criticize nationalism and denominationalism as too narrow and particular. Nor can a relative right be restored to nation and denomination that would override the eschatological awareness of a future world society and religion. A future world religion for unifying mankind is not achieved by idealism (even supposing that such a world religion could be the goal of Christian hope). A world religion might overlook, but it could not eliminate, the problem of radical evil. The burning question of radical evil is not resolved sociopolitically, not even in utopia, nor by making heaven the answer, nor even in resignation.

V. *Political Theology of the Cross Versus Political Idolatry*

In 1935, E. Peterson, countering C. Schmitt, wanted "to prove from a concrete case that a political theology was theologically impossible." From among all the early Christian struggles, Peterson picked out, surprisingly, only two things: the trinitarian critique of imperialism and the eschatological critique of the Christianizing of the Pax Augusta. However, he has shown elsewhere that the early Christian martyrology was a theology of the cross. This placed the crucifixion at the center of the Christian conflict with the Empire. Moreover, the crucifixion is the single public political act in the life of Jesus. Today, the question of the political consequences of the cross has not yet been explicated. To uncover these consequences requires a Christological starting point. This will yield a critical method for both the Church against the political world, and the believer against the Church's own political and social reality. This theology of the cross, therefore, cannot possibly be clerical.

The Christological starting point is that Jesus was condemned as a blasphemer by Israel's law. Pauline and Reformation theology constantly stressed the fact that Jesus died under the law. The power of his resurrection and exaltation put an end to the claims of the law: since Jesus, the Christ of God, was condemned under the law, no man can be justified and liberated by the works of the law, but only by faith. The one accursed by the law became for all the godless the source of faith that sets free and of hope that vivifies. The Reformation theology of the cross found its inspiration in Luther's Heidelberg disputation of 1518. Here, Luther took his stand against natural man's justification by works and even his longing for natural theology. Luther began to draw out the ontological consequences of God's revelation in Christ crucified. Ernst Jüngel has also pointed out how the crucifixion, understood as revelation, contains a specific "ontological tendency."

A merely theological interpretation of the political proceedings against Jesus and the fact that he was not stoned but crucified by the Romans fails as an attempt to draw out the political consequences of the revelation of God in the crucifixion. From a historical point of view, one may speak of the "error in justice" by the Roman garrison, for Jesus was not a Jewish freedom-fighter against Rome. Nevertheless, Jesus' eschatological message of freedom was implicitly a total attack on the very existence of the religious state. In this sense, his crucifixion had political implications; it was not merely fortuitous. The following quotation shows that Hegel saw these implications. For him the death of Jesus was the antithesis to all human institutions and to the very foundations of society.

Since, accordingly, the death . . . is . . . the most degrading of all deaths, death upon the cross involves not only what is natural, but also civil degradation, worldly dishonor; the cross is transfigured, what according to the common idea is lowest, what the State characterises as degrading, is transformed into what is highest. . . . But since degradation is made the highest honor, all those ties that bind human society together are attacked in their foundations, are shaken and dissolved. When the cross has been elevated to the place of a banner, and is made a banner in fact, the positive content of which is at the same time the Kingdom of God, inner feeling is in the very heart of its nature detached from civil and state life, and the substantial basis of this latter is taken away, so that the whole structure has no longer any reality, but is an empty appearance, which must soon come crashing down, and make manifest that it is no longer anything having inherent existence.[5]

Those who recognize God in the crucified one see the glory of God only in the face of Christ crucified and no longer in nature, reason, or political achievements. Glory no longer rests upon the heads of the mighty. For believers, Christ crucified was made the righteousness of God, and for them political authority was deprived of its religious sanction. Christ, crucified in powerlessness and shame, has become their highest authority. Consequently, they no longer believe in religiopolitical authority, for the anxiety and fear that demanded it has been eliminated.

Modern political theology considers the mortal conflict of Jesus with the public powers of his day to be central. Such conflict played no part in the old political theology that developed a "state metaphysics." The only question is how this conflict of Jesus with the public powers can today be expressed in individual Christian practice and ecclesial public life. To work this out in theory alone accomplishes nothing; the opposition must be named specifically. This critical engagement brings us to that area we have called political or civil religion. Here the political theology of the cross is a critical and theoretical instrument for freeing men from political idolatry, paternalism, and alienation. As A. Schlatter said, "therefore the vocation and the work of Jesus consists in destroying our idols by the power of the cross with which he annihilates our false deities." Now there are few spheres of life so riddled with idolatry and alienation as politics. We must, therefore, examine how this liberation can happen.

We will do this by presenting two theses:

1. The Second Commandment, which forbids all images of God, not only initiates a world view freed from ontocracy—as G. Von Rad points out—but a political life freed from idolatry. What the Bible calls "idolatry" is designated in modern critiques as "alienation" and "paternalism."[6]

2. The theology of the cross radically carries through the prohibition of images (a) by demythologizing the ideas of theology, (b) by desacralizing every claim of divinity in man or nature or

natural theology and (c) by fundamentally democratizing government. These things usher in eschatological freedom, for the messianic future of God on earth begins, according to the Jewish prayer,
"when Thou wilt remove idols from the earth, and the nongods
shall be wholly destroyed."[7]

Idolatry, superstition, fetishism, worship of heroes, etc. derive,
according to the Second Commandment, from man's fashioning
visible images of the invisible but audible God. By subordinating
himself to his own handiwork man protects and reassures himself.
Von Rad has shown that in oriental religions, the images are not
simply made by man. Rather, they express a consciousness of
cosmic holiness, a consciousness that views every region of the
world as theophanous and a medium linking gods and men. The
Second Commandment, by forbidding the fashioning of images,
drew the world of nature away from this divine provenance and into
the responsibility of man. It freed man from cultic sanctuaries,
calendars, and images dependent on the natural environment. The
Second Commandment, then, protected and preserved for man his
dominion over creation, for man alone is made in the image and
likeness of God.

This liberating work of the Second Commandment, according to
H. W. Wolff, is continued in prophetic literature as the battle between Yahweh and the gods. This God who is present to history
in his promises liberated man from the idols man himself created to
relieve his burden of responsibility. Deutero-Isaiah insisted that
idols are the product of men's hands and, therefore, they cannot
save their own creator.

For Israel, idolatry was the worst sin and Paul (Rom. 1:18*ff.*)
took up this critique and even transformed it in his analysis of
justification by works. Man not only makes images of gods and so
serves the creature instead of the creator, but also divinizes everything that he does in order to appear to live righteously, compelled
to do this by his desire for self-justification. Therefore, argues Paul,
justification by works is idolatry. Men become the slaves of their
own good works which in their turn justify or condemn those
who do them. What God alone can give, man seeks from his own
works. In this way, the creators bow down before their own creations. The works make the person, not the person the works.

Luther applied Paul's doctrine to the Second Commandment in his Larger Catechism. He related the veneration of images to justification by works and went on to explain that the underlying cause of all sin is idolatry in the heart. He internalized the concept of idolatry by locating it not only in the worship of idols but preeminently in the heart that seeks help and comfort from creatures, saints and devils but "receives not God Himself." "Where you hang your heart," said Luther, "there is your God."

Considered psychologically, from his almost unfathomable anxiety man creates symbols, idols, and values that he identifies with himself. Friedrich Engels went so far as to say that man's anxiety over his existence was the essence of the state and of religion. Every attack upon man's idols is, therefore, lethal; hence man opposes such attacks with deadly aggression. As long as man clings to such idols, he remains unfree to affirm simultaneously his own existence and the very different life of another. This inner compulsion to idolize the self is a cramping self-justification that invariably leads to the oppression of those who are "other." Rational enlightenment alone cannot dispel completely this aggressive idolatry. Emancipation from idolatry requires a new motivation, a new direction to life. Hence, stoic equanimity makes little sense as a replacement for idolatry. Such equanimity may remove man's aggressiveness, but it makes him hardhearted, able to live neither in fear nor in hope. All things are alike to such a man, for he has become incapable of love.

If idolatry consists in the absolutizing of a relative good, still its abolition must not lead to stoic indifference. Selfish love is overcome only in love of another; superstition is removed only by a faith which, freeing, makes possible selfless love. Otherwise an "enlightened" man becomes all too quickly a wizened old man. Self-justification always includes righteousness, but in a perverse form. Idolatry always includes faith, but in a despairing and hybrid form. Selfish love is love, but love that destroys the life it so desperately wants to preserve. Who can cast down the idols man continually fashions so that they do not rise again? A God who guides man to the lordship of creation, who justifies those who are unable to justify themselves, who makes possible selfless love for those whom He loves. For theology to work out the practical significance of these ideas, it must relate itself to the Enlightenment program of critical reason aiming to effect the liberation of mankind. In practicing the iconoclasm of the Second Commandment, Christian belief and critical Enlightenment share a common cause.

The critical sciences of the Enlightenment have perpetuated the liberating results of the Second Commandment, even when theology and the church have contributed little to this process. Here we are paralleling the modern critique of ideology with the biblical ban on images. It is reasonable, then, to relate the Christian kerygma and doctrine to the history of freedom since the Enlightenment. The synthesis of theology and political practice occurs in the sphere of political and ethical reason. This sphere, at the institutional and ideological level, is a mixture of actualized freedoms and continuing oppressions.

Bacon unmasked traditional biases as *idola*—images of god— that so enthralled men's minds that empirical truth could hardly enter. When truth did enter, these idols returned to impede the scientific renaissance. Kant penetrated the "dogmatism of reason" by a critical reflection on the conditions of the possibility of theoretical reason. Feuerbach's critique of religious projection intended specifically to promote man's cultural and historical coming of age. But it can also be understood (as Adorno shows) as the carrying out of the Second Commandment and as "negative theology." It need scarcely be noted that Freud's psychoanalysis is to a great extent an "enlightenment" regarding the psychological mechanisms of idolatry. And it is noteworthy that Marx identified his critique of religion as the "beginning of every critique." Marx's analysis of religion is an analysis of idolatry: "The offspring of their minds have overwhelmed them. The creators have bowed down before their creatures."[8] Marx's analysis of both religion and capitalism follow this principle. These works mold the person, producing religious as well as social alienation. The category of possessing overshadows the category of being. In Marx's later writings on the "fetish character" of goods in barter societies, his earlier critique of religion reappeared. If Christian theology neglects this Enlightenment critique of superstition and idolatry, it only injures itself.

It was Hobbes, not theologians, who interpreted the Second Commandment politically: That they should not make any image to represent them, that is to say, they were not to choose to themselves, neither in heaven, nor in earth, any representative of their own fancying (*Leviathan*, chapter 42). This quotation brings us to the problem of political representation. Political representation is essential for a people seeking the political power to shape their own history (E. Voegelin). The political community organizes itself on the lines of a theater with its stage of public life on which representatives play their parts. The citizens, like the audience, identify with their representatives and with their representatives' decisions. They delegate to their representatives certain rights of self-determination and authorize them to act in their name. The danger of alienation always accompanies this indispensable process; indeed, alienation is inevitable. Norman Brown has pointed out that "in representative institutions there is always subjection to the visible image: idolatry"[9] Political idolatry and political alienation occur when the representatives rise above their constituents and when their constituents bend the knee before them. The result is seen in growing political apathy. The constituents can no longer identify with their representatives nor endorse their decisions. They fall into passivity because the representatives are out of control and this indifference only accelerates the misuse of power. I believe the following are the symptoms of political idolatry: delegation leads to domination, representation to alienation, functional rule to absolute authority.

The republicans of the Enlightenment saw very clearly the connection between idolatry, political alienation, and paternalism. The fourth president of the United States, John Quincy Adams, said, "Democracy has no monuments. It strikes no medals. It does not bear the head of a man on its coinage. Its true character is iconoclast." If this is the true character of a democracy, then its reality consists in the continual revision of established political forms, and in promoting the people's share in participation in and control of the government. Therefore, democracy tends to produce public freedom and public happiness. It is the political fulfillment of the Second Commandment. Correlatively, the political execution of the Second Commandment must lead towards democratization.

Iconoclasm is not intelligible in itself but only in relation to something else. In the churches, iconoclasm should clear away the images to make room for the gospel in man's history. In politics, iconoclasm should set men free to accept responsibility. In its critique of ideology, iconoclasm should loose the utopian power of fantasy, so that men may imagine better social relations in the future. As mere theoretical critique, however, iconoclasm degenerates into empty irony—an abstract antithesis which, ironically, can coexist with each and every ideology and idolatry.

The prohibition of idols specifically differentiates Israel from its neighbors. In the same way, Christianity is properly also called the religion of the cross. Belief in the lordship of Christ crucified differentiates Christianity from other religions and ideologies. The cross separates belief from unbelief and superstition. Belief in Christ crucified occupies that space claimed and opened up by the Old Testament's prohibition of images. Only Christ crucified is called "the image of the living God"; belief in him implies the abandonment and destruction of all earthly images and representations of the divine. How is that done?

The Christ of God was executed in the name of religiopolitical authority, an authority supposedly established "from above." Therefore, any justification of authority "from above" no longer is convincing to Christians. Political authority can only receive its justification "from below." Before the time of Christianity, all political theory sought to confirm the status quo. Since Christianity, all political theory should seek to criticize the nature, limits, and purpose of the state. We will draw some examples from the Christian political tradition. The early Church rejected the cult of Caesar and replaced the prayers *to* Caesar with prayers *for* Caesar, asking that his power should know its limits. The Reformation regarded the political structures as divinely permitted; they no longer saved men, but merely sustained a passing world. Christians should permit themselves to be ruled as though they were not ruled (1 Cor. 7). The Puritans destroyed the status quo and class structure and replaced it with a social contract, constitution, or covenant of free citizens. "The crown rests on the constitution" (Thomas Paine). Christians today should again take the lead in secularizing, relativizing and democratizing politics if they want to be consistent. This means that the Church's task of liberating men from idolatry through faith must deal with social, economic, political, and racial alienation—as well as with religious alienation. Churches must be shaken to their foundations and become institutions of sociocritical freedom (as Metz has demanded). It is, however, impossible to eliminate religious idolatry while one is aligned with a political or an economic idolatry. Conversely, it is impossible to criticize political and economic idolatry when religious alienations remain untested. How can these criticisms of idolatry and alienation be carried out?

In a moving passage from his "Lectures on Romans" (1516), Luther has examined this religious alienation by contrasting the "God of hope" with the "gods of tangible reality."

> Now the God of hope fill you with all joy and peace in believing, that you may abound in hope and in the power of the Holy Spirit (Rom 15:13).
> It is strange to call God a "God of hope." But this is the sign by which the apostle distinguishes the false gods from the true God. The false gods are demons and as such they are the gods of tangible reality. They possess them that do not know what it means to hope because they depend upon external things. But he that depends on the true God has laid all tangible things aside and lives by naked hope. To call God "the God of hope" is therefore the same as to call him the God of hopers. He certainly is not the God but the enemy and judge of people who despair easily and are unable to trust anyone.
> In short, he is the "God of hope" because he is the Giver of hope, and, even more, because only hope worships him . . . for where hope is, there one worships him (*ubi spes est ibi cultus est*).[10]

In conclusion, the God of hope disengages himself from the gods of tangible realities who are no more than idols. This disengagement is wrought by the cross of the risen Christ. Therefore, the theology of the cross is the theology of hope; and the theology of hope is a theology of the cross.

VI. *The Political Theology of the Cross and the Church of the "Others"*

The political theology of the cross has still deeper dimensions. It would be myopic to concentrate only on church-state relations with the hope of changing their relationship from one of mutual reinforcement to one of critical distance. The theology of the cross remains abstract if we only think about it in this context. According to its biblical traditions, the Church everywhere has to be with those for whom there is neither state nor status. The Christian faith founded on the cross must begin again to demythologize the state in which it lives. This will succeed only if it concomitantly analyzes the religious situation of those who, according to the present order of things, have no status. Christianity was not founded as a national religion. Its "Deus crucifixus" is a "stateless God." But even though its God is stateless, Christianity did not originate as a private religion and its God is not an "apolitical God."

From the beginning of Israel's history, Yahweh was known as the God of the poor. This tradition runs through Israel's history despite its convenantal and national institutions: "For thou art God of the lowly, helper of the oppressed, upholder of the weak, protector of the forlorn, savior of those without hope (Judith 9:11).

In Mary's Magnificat, the rich and the poor are contrasted: "He has put down the mighty from their thrones, and exalted those of low degree; he has filled the hungry with good things and the rich he has sent empty away" (Luke 1:46–54). Jesus proclaimed "the kingdom of God to the poor." His beatitudes apply to the poor, those in mourning, the hungry, the persecuted and the pure of heart. Paul preached justification by grace alone to the slaves and sinners. In the congregation that assembled around this message he saw the electing and condemning God at work: the weak, the lowly, the destitute, the despised were elected through the word of the cross. This same word revealed the disgrace of those who considered themselves strong, noble, rich, and important (1 Cor 1: 26–28). "The poor alone rejoice in the good news." This good news was a stumbling block to the rich.

It would be a misunderstanding to think that the promise given to those who have nothing in this world means their compensation after death and their riches in heaven. Quite the opposite is true. The poor do not go to the kingdom of God, rather the kingdom of God comes to the poor. The kingdom of God begins in this world with the poor; the justice of God comes justifying those who are suffering from injustice. The new future promised by God begins not in the "beyond" but in the appearance of the Son of Man among the neglected. This new future of God is not some "vanguard of social progress and cultural development," rather, it belongs to those who are in the dark and therefore overlooked. With the cross, the future of God allies itself with those whom a self-satisfied and conformist society has reduced to nothing. In this way, there arises a real "messianism of the oppressed." The oppressed are no longer the object of the charity of the rich (nor recipients of aid in developing nations), but are themselves custodians of the law and redeemers of the rich. The rich do not save the poor, the poor save the rich. How can this happen?

Only the poor know the oppression of exclusion from riches. Only the humiliated know the pain of humiliation. Only the hated know the wretchedness of hatred. Conversely, the rich, the oppressors, and the haters are unknowing and blind, even if they are of good will. They unconsciously live in terms of an objective communal delusion (Marx) and despite their own effort and critical theory, they manage to remain blind to the way things really are. The oppressed hold in their hand the key for the liberation of mankind from oppression.

Those who in a given society are the "others"—Jews, blacks, poor, slaves, "widows and orphans"—will, as outcasts, know their true plight before God. These cannot appear to be other than they really are. They are abandoned, left without protection, nothing. In them is revealed the real condition of man before God. Israel was taught its estranged and straying condition before Yahweh by the presence of strangers and wanderers in their midst. In Matthew 25, the Son of Man who comes to judge the world identifies himself with the hungry, the imprisoned, the naked, and the persecuted by calling them his "least brethren." This has nothing to do with being nice to neighbors, for these "least brethren" are in no way nearby, but are condemned to distance. Hence, these "least brethren" are never our "neighbors."

The teaching in Matthew 25 does not belong to social ethics, but primarily to ecclesiology. He who sees in Christ crucified the presence of God belongs to the hidden brotherhood of Christ. This man is identified with the downtrodden and sees himself in them because and insofar as he sees Christ in them. Where, then, is the Church of Christ? The old maxim affirms that the true Church is there where Christ is: *"Ubi Christus—ibi ecclesia."* The New Testament theology of the Church contains two series of promises which point out the presence of Christ. The first refers to the word, the sacrament, and the fellowship in faith: "Who hears you hears me." This is the Church representing the risen Christ to the world. The second is expressed in the sayings: "What you have done to the least of my brethren this you do unto me"; "who visits them visits me." These sayings point to Christian hope in the world and delineate the area of human life where Christ is present. The Church exists, therefore, as a twofold brotherhood: those who are sent and those who are waiting. The former is the manifest and visible brotherhood of believers; the latter is the latent and hidden brotherhood of the poor. The former belongs to the resurrection, the latter, to the fellowship of the cross. The Christian church is not coextensive with the Church of Christ as long as it cannot express this twofold brotherhood. The Church would be false if, in the spirit of triumphalism, it represented only the risen Lord and claimed to be the kingdom of God. The Church, because of Christ crucified, should search out and identify with those whom Christ by his suffering and death took as brothers. It can only credibly preach the gospel as a "call to freedom" (Käsemann) if it utters the "cry for freedom" of those reduced to silence. Is there not some justice in J. Cone's contention in *Black Theology* that it should be theologically possible in the twentieth century to see Christ as black as it was in the first century to see him as Jew?

This ecclesiology does not mean that the oppressed should become the oppressor. For the gospel reconciles all sinners. It must penetrate all social divisions and all political manifestations of self-justification made at the expense of another. Otherwise it remains abstract and ineffectual. Insofar as the gospel praises the poor as blessed and promises them the kingdom of God, it saves the rich also by revealing their real poverty. Unless the "subversive" character of the Bible as the "Bible of the poor" pervades eschatology, then the promise of a new and reconciled mankind receives no authentic witness.

Of course, such ideas bring one close to enthusiastic notions of the Church where persecution and suffering are normative signs of the Church (*notae ecclessiae*). Though persecution and suffering are not negative, their presence is not the only characteristic of God's kingdom in this world. The suffering and the persecuted are seen in a new light by the gospel of the crucified Christ. They are not made into instruments of God's vengeance but are empowered to save from dehumanizing oppression both the oppressor and the oppressed.

VII. *Summary*

1. Political, or civil, religion is the integrating symbolism of a nation. It helps to unify the population. It fosters the self-justification of a nation. Through it a nation makes its origin into a myth and glorifies its history. These are the "Dii rei," the gods of political reality.

2. Christian belief in the crucified God who is the God of hope casts down idols, releases men from the compulsion for self-justification, and overthrows the tyranny of pride and fear.

3. The Church of Christ cannot become identified with a national community. It must be a fellowship with the "others," with those who are the victims of tyrannical pride and fear.

4. Liberation from the idolatry of a nation's political religion introduces people to the universal kingdom of God in fellowship with the "others."

5. The freedom of Christian faith transforms a nation's self-justification into solidarity with the victims of its political religion; Christian faith seeks to act as the representative of those who are victimized.

6. Ecclesial institutions cannot persist in their sociopolitical neutrality, nor can they leave social responsibility to individual Christians alone. Moreover, because churches have a certain public respectability and influence, they cannot develop into institutions that exercise genuine social criticism. Only if the churches bind themselves concretely to the lives of the "others" will they free themselves from their alliance with the dominant society and its religious need for self-justification.

As we have seen, genuine "political theology" is unwilling to reduce Christian beliefs to politics or to substitute humanism for

Christianity. If we were in practice to put man in Christ's place, then theoretically we would have to put man on a par with divinity. If we were to transform religion into politics, as our leftist and Marxist friends demand, then politics would be our religion. The state or the party would be Leviathan, a mortal god of the earth. This would run counter to the desacralizing, secularizing, and democratizing of politics effected by Christianity. The worship of politics is a superstition, anathema to Christians. For Christians are joined with Christ crucified to speak to men of a greater freedom.

A Christian "political theology" wants to bring Christians to the point of solidarity, to the place where Christ awaits them. In the suffering and the outcasts of this earth, Christ awaits his own.

Christian hope focuses not simply upon a better future but on the future of the hopeless. The light of the resurrection shines in the night of the cross and will illuminate those who today have fallen under the shadow of the cross. The cross of Christ, the community of the body of Christ, and the sighs of the oppressed creature all point to the one place of authentic Christian presence.

Luther said, "The cross alone is our theology." The thesis of this treatise is: the cross is our political critique, the cross is our hope for a politics of freedom. The memory of Christ crucified compels us to a political theology.

NOTES

1. Herbert Marcuse, *Five Lectures*, chap. 4, "The End of Utopia," trans. J. Shapiro and S. Weber (Boston: Beacon Press, 1970), pp. 68–69.

2. Robert Bellah, "Civil Religion in America," *Daedalus* (1967), reprinted with modifications in *The Religious Situation 1968* (Boston: Beacon Press, 1968), pp. 331–354.

3. James H. Cone, *Black Theology and Black Power* (New York: The Seabury Press, 1969).

4. Peter L. Berger, *The Noise of Solemn Assemblies*: *Christian Commitment and the Religious Establishment in America* (Garden City, N.Y.: Doubleday, 1961).

5. G. W. F. Hegel, *The Philosophy of Religion*, ed. E. Speirs, trans. E. Speirs and J. Sanderson (New York: Humanities Press, 1968), 3:90.

6. Erich Fromm, *The Revolution of Hope: Toward a Humanized Technology* (New York: Harper & Row, 1968).

7. Emil L. Fackenheim, "Idolatry as a Modern Religious Possibility," *The Religious Situation 1968* (Boston: Beacon Press, 1968), pp. 254–287, 256.

8. Karl Marx, *Die Frühschriften*, ed. S. Landshut (1953), p. 341.

9. Norman O. Brown, *Love's Body* (New York: Vintage Books, Random House, 1968), p. 122.

10. Martin Luther, *Lectures on Romans*, The Library of Christian Classics, trans. and ed. W. Pauck (Philadelphia: Westminster Press, 1961), 15:413.

11. Ernst Bloch, *Man on His Own*, trans. E. Ashton (New York: Herder and Herder, 1970).

M. DARROL BRYANT

2. America as God's Kingdom

Introduction by Henry Vander Goot

Introduction

In "America as God's Kingdom," M. Darrol Bryant analyzes the influence of the Great Awakening on American history. He argues that this event, which took place in the early 1740's, is the true American revolution. This revolution was completed in the minds and hearts of the people long before America fought its War of Independence a generation later.

The Great Awakening was, of course, a religious revival. But it was a religious revival that was different from those that preceded it. The special point of difference is this: in the Great Awakening the new feelings and behavior of those who were affected by it were interpreted as signs that the millennium was at hand. They were regarded as evidences that the Holy Spirit was now beginning to establish God's perfect kingdom on earth and to initiate a new age of peace and justice.

In Christian belief, the millennium is the perfect kingdom of God on earth and is imagined to be a 1,000-year reign of peace and justice which will take place at the end of history. Traditionally, it is believed that the millennium will be established by Jesus Christ when he comes again. (This traditional view is called "*pre*millennialism" because it asserts that Jesus Christ will come again *prior* to the millennium.) The political consequence of premillennial belief is to discourage people from identifying any particular historical progress with the beginnings of the kingdom of God on earth and to contradict any claim that a realm of perfect justice can be established by social improvements. This is the case because, from the premillennialist perspective, the sole sign and cause of the millennium is the actual return of the Son of Man.

In colonial America, however, a theological reinterpretation of the millennium was developed. Some began to speculate that Jesus Christ might return again to earth only *after* the millennium had been established. This view is called "*post*millennialism." The political consequence of postmillennialism is to encourage the view that particular historical developments can constitute true progress towards the kingdom of God. This belief also establishes a basis for the claim that events other than the return of Jesus might both signify and effect the beginnings of the millennial age. It is precisely this postmillennialist orientation that allowed certain New Englanders to identify the extraordinary experiences associated with the Great Awakening as signs that the millennium was at hand. The same postmillennialist outlook, still persisting in secular forms today, allows people to believe that America is both the scene and even the agent of the salvation of the world. In its least pernicious form, this belief underwrites the notion that American life is somehow "better," and American political institutions somehow more appropriate to the way God's will is done on earth.

The virtue of Bryant's essay is to distinguish the kinds and consequences of various *eschatologies*—those theories that seek to articulate, in a symbolic manner, the conditions of the fulfillment of the world. Bryant describes postmillennialist eschatology as a "principle of revolutionary criticism," since it initiates social change by describing a perfect social order as something that can be established by particular human actions. He then describes premillennialist eschatology as a "principle of criticism of revolutionary criticism," since it denies the assumption that man can establish God's kingdom (i.e., denies that man can realize his utopian visions). Finally, Bryant outlines the elements of a third eschatology: the "transhistorical" or "antimillennialist" belief that man's fulfillment takes place only in a dimension beyond time and space. The fulfillment of all things is eternal life. The consequence of this third eschatology, suggests Bryant, is to relativize not merely our judgments about man's capacity for righteous action, but even our judgments about his capacity for developing comprehensive theories of history and perfected community. Such millennialist theories, suggests Bryant, are always ideological and expressions of the sinfulness and pride of man. As such, they can never be the foundation of a truly political society. A political society, rather, is based only on a transhistorical eschatology. (See, for example, Herbert Richardson's essay in this volume.)

Essentially, Bryant's essay is dealing with the same problem that Jürgen Moltmann has discussed in "The Cross and Civil Religion." Both writers see that the fundamental problem of modern theology arises in relation to eschatology, and both argue that all millennialist (or historical) eschatologies provide the basis for ideological revolution and the idolatrous overevaluation of particular historical situations. This is no less true when Christian millennialism underwrites American nationalism than it is when pagan eschatology gives rise to Nazism, or "scientific utopianism" spawns Communism. But whereas Moltmann utilized the symbol of the cross to bring such millennialist eschatologies under criticism, Bryant, following Jonathan Edwards, utilizes the symbols of eternal life and the Holy Trinity. Structurally, both essays focus on the same problem and give essentially similar analyses and resolutions, even though the authors utilize somewhat different symbolisms.

America as God's Kingdom

In the life of a people the founding events are the ones continually returned to both in moments of celebration and crisis. A people returns to its beginnings to give thanks and to regain orientation, to recover the faith which inspired its beginnings. In the American experience the events usually returned to are those surrounding the American Revolution. Although this complex of events is worthy of attention—the cast has magnificence, the drama magnitude, and the speech occasional eloquence—exclusive focus here obscures a secret of the American experience. John Adams, an architect of America's political beginnings, gave expression to a puzzle when he wrote: "A history of the first war of the United States is a very different thing from a history of the American Revolution. The Revolution was effected before the war commenced. The Revolution was in the minds and hearts of the people."[1] If the "Revolution" was not centered in the War of Independence then where do we locate it? What was the content of the "Revolution" such that the War of Independence was simply an event within an ongoing process, or a step along the way?

Our contention is that the place to seek for clues to this puzzle is the Great Awakening. That convulsion of colonial America in the 1740s is, we argue, the venture into open time and space. Here is to be found America's Jacob experience, its wrestling with the unnamed powers of heaven and earth to gain a blessing.

In 1740 Nathan Cole, a Connecticut farmer, went to hear George Whitefield preach. He returned home deeply affected. As he wrote in his diary, "My old Foundation was broken up."[2] But that experience of disintegration gave way to a new affirmation as Cole wrote, "Now I saw with new eyes; all things became new."[3] This experience was not Nathan Cole's alone; it was the experience of a generation. Moreover, the breaking up of old foundations and the vision of all things becoming new is the stuff out of which revolutions in the minds and hearts of the people are forged.

Against this background, we can move towards a formulation of a secret of the American experience: crucial aspects of the interior, spiritual and symbolic orientation of the American tradition are forged in a religious nexus. This secret is grounded in the interplay between public space and time (politics) and open space and time (religion). In order for the public order to be reformed, the interior constellation of beliefs, values and images—the symbolic universe—which integrates the public order must be broken apart and then reformulated. This is done through the agency of religion.[4]

Specifically, the argument advanced here is that the millennial spirit of the 1740s is integral to the formation of the American tradition. When this dimension of American experience is brought into focus, a peculiar dynamic and dialectic of the American tradition is made manifest. The eschatological dimension is not extraneous or incidental to the American tradition, but integral. And it is in terms of the interplay between the transcendent and immanent, with its attendant temptation towards idolatry, that the greatness and shabbiness of "America" is to be understood.

Warrant for our contention concerning the intimate, if not illicit, relation between religion and American political beginnings is gained from more recent historical studies. Bernard Bailyn in his masterful *Ideological Origins of the American Revolution* writes that "a major source of ideas and attitudes of the Revolutionary generation stemmed ultimately from the political and social theories of New England Puritanism."[5] Further, he writes that it was the religious tradition which "offered a context for everyday events nothing less than cosmic in its dimensions."[6] It is this "cosmic context" that is our special concern here. Central to this concept is "the idea that America had a special place, as yet not fully revealed, in the architecture of God's intent."[7] This eschatology, to use Bailyn's formulation, "prepared the colonists for a convulsive realization by locating their parochial concerns at a critical juncture on the map of mankind's destiny."[8] Already we come to the heart of the problematic: the presumptuous belief that the American Republic is the realization of an eschatological hope. Is not this the idolatrous assumption which makes the transcendent the underwriter of the political Republic and, thus, transforms Christianity into a civil religion?

This negative formulation of a generic relation between religion and politics in the American tradition can also be stated positively. Robert Bellah, for example, has argued that the consequence of this tradition is "the subordination of the nation to ethical principles that transcend it and in terms of which it should be judged."[9] But such critical considerations run ahead of our analysis. The crucial point here is that the beginnings of the Republic are nurtured within a religious nursery.

The assertion of an interior relationship between religion and politics in the American tradition should come as no surprise. It is part and parcel of the tradition out of which "America" is born. The Puritan forebearers came "on an errand."[10] The sense of special destiny which inaugurated the venture into this new land was articulated by John Winthrop aboard the Arabella in 1630: "Wee shall be a Citty upon a Hill, the eies of all people are uppon us; soe that if wee shal deale falsely with our god in this worke wee have undertaken and soe cause him to withdrawe his present help from us, wee shall be made a story and a by-word through the world."[11] That this religious tradition nurtures the beginnings of American history is crucial in at least two respects. Firstly, the societal vocation is formulated in relation to some transcendent end. Thus an internal dialectic is set up between the promise (what we shall become) and the reality (what is). Simultaneously, a temptation towards the deification of the present is also at hand.[12] Secondly, in the Puritan tradition, Christian vocation is directed not only towards the reformation of the Church but also the reformation of the world. Thus the move from a religious vision to sociopolitical action is intrinsic to this tradition.[13]

Against the backdrop of these historical considerations, we should expect that the Great Awakening was not a narrow ecclesiastical event but one crucial to the whole of societal life. The last decade of research on the Great Awakening is summarized by C. C. Goen when he writes: "The entire epoch of the Great Awakening was . . . a critical juncture where old values were failing and a new order was emerging.[14] Here the Great Awakening comes into view as a watershed event in the formation of the American tradition, a time when fundamental questions were open and critical orientations toward the future established. In one sense, the assertion that the Great Awakening is a secret source of the American tradition is commonplace. Many, for example, credit the Great Awakening with the enhancement of the status of the "common man."[15] As such, it is an influence toward democracy. How does this dynamic work?

The novelty of recent research lies in the emphasis given to the eschatological emphasis within the Great Awakening. Alan Heimert, whose work is especially responsible for recent increased attention to the Great Awakening, writes: "The watershed in American history marked by the 1740s can be understood best in terms of the degree to which, after the Great Awakening, the American populace was filled with the notion of an impending millennium. From 1740 on, American thought and expression—or, more precisely, that of the evangelical American—was above all characterized by a note of expectation."[16] The new "note of expectation" did not arise spontaneously but was born of the labor and travail which comes in wrestling with the heavens to reveal their secret concerning the millennium. The new note of expectation is the affectional consequence of a vision of what the future promises. The question "What *does* the future promise?" is in large measure what is at stake in the controversy over whether or not the Great Awakening was a "prelibation of heaven's glory" or sulfuric fumes from the collapse of this "errand into the wilderness."

Goen's and Heimert's summaries taken together are significant in two respects. Firstly, they rightly restore the Great Awakening to a central place in the formation of America's self-understanding. Secondly, they underscore the centrality of the millennial dynamic in the formation of that self-understanding. This millennial element is the crucial dynamic of that cosmic context which forms the symbolic nexus of the political Republic. Hence, it was an awareness of the interior relation between the Great Awakening and the War of Independence that led Perry Miller to remark that "the American Revolution was a revival which had the astonishing good fortune to succeed."[17] Now the critical, historical question which must be asked is this: What are the historical grounds for such a claim? Can this claim be documented textually or must it finally be taken as an expression of an idolatrous self-understanding of the Republic? Or, perhaps better, is this a statement of an American self-understanding which can be supported by an analysis of those figures appealed to to support such a claim?

We do not claim to be able to answer such questions in their entirety, but we propose to move towards an answer in relation to a specific articulator of America's vocation: Jonathan Edwards. In commenting on the Great Awakening as a critical juncture, Goen writes: "Jonathan Edwards proved to be a charismatic leader for that moment of *kairos* in American history when a bewildered people groped uncertainly to recapture their faltering sense of destiny.[18] In Heimert's study of the relationship between the Great Awakening and the American Revolution, Jonathan Edwards is continually appealed to to document his case. In commenting upon Edwards' outline of a work never completed, *A History of the Work of Redemption*, Heimert writes: "So accurately did it delineate the course which American society would take that it might be called a scenario for American social and political history in the last half of the eighteenth century.[19] Thus, Edwards is appealed to as a major architect of the American tradition, the one who more than anyone else grounded the vocation of America within the divine economy.

This view of Edwards has a precedent. The nineteenth-century American historian, George Bancroft, likewise credits Edwards with the initial formulation of America's vocation.[20] That formulation is theological—unfortunately, in Bancroft's eyes—but it is nevertheless there. Bancroft's scant comments amount to a view of America as fulfilling a moral role in world history beyond meaner economic and political considerations. Heimert's position is not nearly so explicit as Bancroft's, but it trades on the same assumption, namely, that America is the Republic born out of the War of Independence. This is the assumption that we wish to call into question.

Our inquiry now falls into two parts. Firstly, we want to affirm the interior relationship between the Great Awakening and the

American Revolution, i.e., the fact that the millennial expectation of a dawning new age served as the ground for a revolutionary critique of the old order and as the dynamic for social innovation. Secondly, we want to argue that on historical grounds, the assumption that the millennial impulse gains fulfillment in the American Republic is unwarranted, at least in relation to Jonathan Edwards. And we shall argue, on theological grounds, that such an identification involves an idolatrous confusion of the politics of God and the politics of man.

I. *Eschatology as a Principle of Revolutionary Criticism*

On the eve of the Great Awakening, New England seemed to have lost her commanding sense of vocation. Perry Miller observes concerning the works of Thomas Foxcroft and Thomas Prince, published at the end of New England's first century, 1730: "Both present history within the frame of the covenant, both portray the covenanting fathers as men of ideal piety, both survey the mighty things God hath wrought for his chosen people, the wonderful deliverances—and then both turn into jeremiads, castigating the declension, apostasy, ingratitude, and corruption in which a century now finds America."[21] The works of Foxcroft and Prince reveal the critical shift in temporal vision from the future to the past. What had happened to Winthrop's vision of a "citty set upon a hill?" Passion towards the future seemed to have withered; instead, the "Golden Age" was now in the past as something remembered, not something hoped for. If faith was orientation towards the future, then faith had faltered. Thus the religious tradition was in serious difficulties, and with it, the society. For in this tradition the corporate, social vision was intimately related to the religious symbolization of the future.

The societal malaise was augmented by other considerations as well. Increasing commerce, population, and material prosperity had pushed beyond the boundaries of primary, face-to-face communities to the more complex world of towns within an economic network.[22] The period from inside, writes Miller, was "a complex of tensions and anxieties."[23] The social boat which normally transports a generation from the shore of birth to the shore of death was being swamped. External contradictions of social life were matched by internal disorientation in the life of the populace.

Jonathan Edwards' personal biography runs parallel to that of the social history of this period. Born in East Windsor, Connecticut, in 1703, he attended Yale and served as a minister of a Presbyterian church in New York City from 1722 to 1723. Returning to Yale as a tutor in 1724, he was installed as pastoral assistant to his aging grandfather, Solomon Stoddard, in Northampton in 1726. Three years later Stoddard died, and at the age of twenty-six Jonathan Edwards became head pastor of the Northampton congregation. Northampton was not just another inland parish. Under the leadership of Stoddard it had come to play a central, if not dominant role in the social, economic, and ecclesiastical affairs of the Connecticut River Valley.[24]

Thus Edwards had been exposed to, indeed he lived in the midst of these gathering "tensions and anxieties." And, like many pious men before him, he sought to discern the "signs of the times." The apocalyptic literature of the Bible, particularly the book of Revelations, was, we now know, the focus of much of his search for some insight, some vision, into the meaning of the events which threatened his life and the lives of those who, by virtue of his office, he was committed to care for and lead. Among the literary remains is an unpublished "Apocalyse" over 200 pages in length and spanning thirty-five years. S. J. Stein writes concerning this material that "in 1723, at age 19, Jonathan Edwards drew together his thoughts on the book of Revelation and gave expression to his belief that the millennium was near."[25] In these private manuscripts, we gain a picture of Jonathan Edwards brooding over contemporary affairs and searching for the key to their meaning in a developing providential view of history. These manuscripts are important in a formal sense: the exploration of the apocalyptic materials and the articulation of an historical theory were correlated with the quest for an understanding of contemporary affairs.

C. C. Goen argues that the Great Awakening "marks the inauguration of the revival tradition in America."[26] But then he acknowledges that under Stoddard, Edwards' predecessor, Northampton had been the scene of the five "harvests." His description is, therefore, misleading. More adequate to the textual materials would be a description of the Great Awakening that distinguishes it from the earlier revivals in terms of the eschatological orientation of the Awakening.

The crucial transition in Edwards' understanding of the revival phenomenon is obvious when we compare his writings on the Connecticut River Valley events of 1734–35 with his writings on the Great Awakening. In the *Five Discourses*, sermons preached during the earlier revival and published at the behest of his congregation, a sermon entitled "Pressing into the Kingdom" reveals no innovative eschatology.[27] Likewise, in *A Faithful Narrative of the Surprising Work of God in the Conversion of Many Hundred Souls in Northampton*,[28] published first in London in 1737 and in Boston in 1738, one searches in vain for the kinds of eschatological materials one finds in *Some Thoughts Concerning the Present Revival of Religion in New England*,[29] published in 1742. The *Faithful Narrative* is, however, significant in another respect. For here one finds Edwards ecstatic over the power of this "surprising work of God" to transform the life of a town. In a letter to Benjamin Colman, Edwards wrote: "In the spring and summer following, *anno* 1735, the town seemed to be full of the presence of God, full of love and joy so as never before."[30] And in the *Faithful Narrative*: "Our converts then remarkably appeared united in dear affection to one another and many have expressed much of that spirit of love which they felt toward mankind; and particularly to those that had been least friendly to them."[31] The very suspicion that this might be tied to some world transforming event Edwards explicitly rejects. "There have also been reports spread about the country . . . that the world was near to an end, which was altogether a false report.[32] Rather he affirms the basic continuity of the 1734–35 revival with the work of his grandfather. "The work that has now been wrought on souls is evidently the same that was wrought in my venerable predecessor's days."[33] This awakening is surely something to rejoice in and Edwards does when he concludes: "And we are evidently a people blessed of the Lord! And here, in this corner of the world, God dwells and mainfests his glory."[34] This joyful, but restrained, exclamation stands in marked contrast to what we will see in *Some Thoughts*.

As one moves from these earlier writing to the writings of the Great Awakening, one sees that the focus shifts from the town of Northampton to the whole of colonial society and even to the whole of humankind. This enlarged sociological context required a correspondingly wider vision. The period between the 1734–35 revival and the Great Awakening marks a crucial transition for Edwards.

The relevant textual evidence of this transition is found in Edwards' sermons of 1738–39 which were not published until 1774 as *A History of the Work of Redemption*.[35] Here we have in outline a projected work which remained uncompleted. It was to be a major work of divinity "in a new key." Though the mere outline of a book, it is more than 400 pages in length. And it is here that we find the metahistorical vision which was to inform Edwards' reading of the Great Awakening and the backdrop for Edwards' understanding of America's world historical vocation.

Edwards' *History of the Work of Redemption* has received little attention by his major interpreters. Peter Gay sees it as a confirmation of the "medieval" caste of Edwards' mind.[36] That judgment rests upon an Enlightenment view of history and thus tells us more about Gay's commitments than it does about Edwards' work. Earlier C. C. Goen published an article which credits Edwards' *History* with being "new departure in eschatology."[37] That innovation, writes Goen, consisted of a millennial expectation where "Edwards foresaw a golden age for the church on earth, within history, and achieved through the ordinary processes of propagating the gospel in the power of the Holy Spirit."[38] It is against this background that Edwards' eschatology enters the Great Awakening for here, Goen writes, "He began to entertain the idea that God might have purposed to realize the biblical prophecies in America as a land destined to accomplish the renovation of the world."[39] Before we can further explore this interpretation it is crucial to understand the literary character of Edwards' work.

From a literary point of view, *A History of the Work of Redemption* is, to use Northrop Frye's phrase, an encyclopedic myth, or what we have called a "metahistorical vision."[40] The function of such kinds of literature is to provide orientation, or, in societal terms, to focus the energies of a people. In primitive societies it was the function of myth to bring the ordinary life of the tribe into line with the life of the gods; tribal life was a repetition of the primal acts of the gods. Such myths were founded on a cyclical understanding of time. When, however, time is historicized, myth is transformed accordingly.[41] That is to say, temporal activity is still undergirded by a myth but now an eschatological myth. In the Christian tradition that myth is the kingdom of God towards which all history moves and in which gains its fulfillment. Rather than locating the myth in the past, in the archetypal acts of creation, it is placed at the end.

When viewed in this context, the *History* is not, as Gay argues, just "bad history" but is something quite different. In its concern to discern the rhythm of divine activity in history, it creates a "cosmos." Thus disorientation is overcome, a people can move confidently into a future secured by a divine promise. The whole historical process is at once ordered and yet opened out. History is, Edwards writes, "all one work, one design." And that design is the "work of Redemption."

Concerning this world, Edwards writes that "It was doubtless created to be a stage upon which this great and wonderful work of redemption should be transacted."[42] The historical process is rendered transparent when the design or rhythm of that work of redemption is grasped. And that design is dramatically revealed in Christ. Writes Edwards: "It is but one design that is formed, to which all the offices of Christ directly tend, and in which all the persons of the Trinity conspire. All the various dispensations that belong to it are united; and the several wheels are one machine, to answer one end, and produce one effect.[43] The intention here is not to deny history but to affirm the unity of the historical process and to render it transparent.

Like his Puritan fathers, Edwards grounds his eschatological vision in the covenant. It is the fulfillment of God's "covenant-promises" which is the substance of history. Miller has written that the "covenant" is conspicuously absent in Edwards' work. While that is true of some of Edwards' earlier writing, it is not accurate here. By grounding his eschatology in the "covenant-promises" Edwards undergirds the certitude of the believer, the twistings and turnings of history notwithstanding. It is God's righteousness which will prevail, not man's strivings. Writes Edwards: "By God's righteousness is here meant his faithfulness in fulfilling his covenant-promises to his church, or, his faithfulness to his church and people, in bestowing the benefits of the covenant of grace upon them."[44]

Though the ecclesiastical community has a unique status in rela-

tion to the work of Redemption, it is crucial to recall that that
vocation is for the sake of the whole body or humankind. This
danger Goen courts when he speaks of "a golden age for the church
on earth."[45] Heimert runs into rough water on another side when
he claims Edwards *History* is "a scenario for American social and
political history in the last half of the eighteenth century."[46] In
this judgment, Heimert transforms the eschatological myth into a
divine sanction for a particular history. Neither option is warranted.
As Edwards' writes, "God's design was *to restore the ruins of the
fall*, and therefore we read of the restitution of all things." Or, "But
the design of God was to restore all, and as it were to create a new
heaven and a new earth."[48] Such a vision is not intended as an
historical blueprint, but to undergird the life of faith come what
may. And more, to encourage the faithful to rest in the divine
promise.

The divine work of Redemption has design. What is that design?
Here Edwards enumerates five "main things . . . to be accomplished."[49]

[1] It is to put all God's enemies under his feet, and that *his goodness
may appear triumphant over all evil.* [50]
[2] God's design was *to restore the ruins of the fall*, and therefore we
read of the restitution of all things.[51]
[3] . . . "*to gather together in one all things in Christ*, in heaven and
in earth," and to unite all in one body of God the Father.[52]
[4] . . . to perfect and complete the *glory of all the elect by Christ*.[53]

And, finally, a work which is not distinct from the others, but simply
summarizes the whole and denotes its telos, namely (5) "to accomplish the *glory of the blessed Trinity*."[54] In one sense, this is
simply traditional Christian faith. The themes are familiar: conflict,
restoration, unity, and consummation. Such a design orients consciousness and activity in the world; it provides a symbolic structure for receiving the world and acting in it. This design acknowledges conflict but affirms the hope for triumph; it recognizes the
broken character of life but seeks its restoration; it knows of dis-
unity but works towards unification; it recognizes imperfection but
strives for fulfillment. Such a mythic structuring of consciousness
undergirds life in the world. It becomes the structure in terms of
which historical life is read and acted.

A perception of God's design is crucial for human being-in-the-world. Without such a perception we wander aimlessly, without orientation. Elsewhere Edwards observes:

> As man is made capable of knowing his Creator, so he is capable of knowing his will in many things, i.e., he is capable of knowing his ends in this and the other works of his, which he beholds. For it is this way principally that he comes to know there is a God, even by seeing the final cause of things; by seeing that such and such things are plainly designed and contrived for such and such ends; and therefore he is capable of either complying with the will of his Creator, or opposing it.[55]

In other words, the task of human imagination is to perceive the design, learn its rhythms and to act in conformity to it. Or as Edwards writes in the *Work of Redemption*: "it is fit that mankind should be somewhat informed of God's design in the government of the world, because they are made capable of actively falling in with that design, or promoting it, and acting herein as his friends and subjects."[56] These words run directly counter to Heimert's claim that "the Calvinist [here he has been citing Edwards] view of history was a stirring reminder that man's own efforts, God willing and assisting, were the only means of advancing the Kingdom."[57] To the contrary, Edwards affirms the priority of divine initiative. That the manifold events of history will be woven into the seamless garment which is the work of Redemption, Edwards affirms. Indeed, he even claims it to be reasonable to suppose

> that there is some great design to which Providence subordinates all the great successive changes in the world which he has made; that all revolutions, from the beginnings of the world to the end, are but the various parts of the scheme, all conspiring to bring about that great event which the Creator and Governor of the world has ultimately in view; and that the scheme will not be finished, nor the design fully accomplished till the end of the world, and the last revolution is brought about.[58]

For Edwards, it is God who moves history. And it the first duty of ministers, "above all others," he writes in *Some Thoughts*, "that they should have understanding of the times and know what Israel ought to do."[59] Thus it is not human effort "God willing and

assisting" which advances the kindom, but man responding in conformity to what God is initiating upon the stage where the "great
and wonderful work of Redemption" is being transacted. This
crucial distinction is easily swamped, as the Great Awakening itself
was to prove to Edwards' deep dismay.

God's plan is being accomplished historically, Edwards asserts.
This history may be roughly divided into three periods: (1) from
the Fall to the Incarnation; (2) from Christ's Incarnation to the
Resurrection; (3) from Christ's Resurrection to the end of the
world.[60] For our investigation, the relevant material is found in
the section dealing with the period from Christ's Resurrection to
the end of the world. Almost half of the work falls into this section
which contains a tour of world history up to the present as well as
prophetic speculation from the "present to the fall of the Anti-
Christ." It is in relation to these materials that Edwards is called
"America's first postmillennial thinker."[61]

As a postmillennial thinker, Edwards believes in a time prior to
Christ's return when "Satan's visible kingdom on earth shall be
utterly overthrown."[62] Although preceded by "*a very dark time*
with respect to the interests of religion in the world,"[63] this "great
work of God will be wrought, though very swiftly, yet gradually."[64]
The primary means of this work shall be through "the wonderful
revival and propagation of religion,"[65] which will be met by "violent
and mighty opposition."[66] The overthrow of Satan's kingdom will
entail, among other things, the abolishment of "heresies, infidelity,
and superstition,"[67] the overthrow of the Mohammedan kingdom,[68]
and the overcoming of "Jewish infidelity."[69] The plus side of the
ledger includes "a time of great light and *knowledge*,"[70] "great *holiness*,"[71] "*great peace and love*"[72] in which "all the world shall be
united in one amiable society. All nations in all parts of the world,
on every side of the globe, shall then be knit together in sweet
harmony. All parts of God's church shall assist and promote the
spiritual good of one another."[73] Edwards lists in all nine features
of this glorious time, a time which ends with apostasy and then the
general Judgment. It is this cosmological vision that Edwards
preached on the eve of the Great Awakening and, thus, inspired
his hearers to look to the future with great expectations. Like his
predecessors in this idiom he does not fix a timetable to his

prophetic ruminating but rather holds it up as an occasion for faith. He concludes: "Let all who are in a Christless condition seriously consider these things, and not be like the foolish people of the old world, who would not take warning . . . and so were consumed in that terrible destruction."[74]

In the course of events from the Reformation to the present, an event of considerable import is the discovery of America. But its significance is in relation to the propagation of the gospel. Edwards writes: "I think we may well look upon the discovery of so great a part of the world, and bringing the Gospel into it, as one thing by which divine Providence is preparing the way for the future glorious times of the church, when Satan's kingdom shall be overthrown throughout the whole habitable globe, on every side, and on all its continents."[75] Thus America is taken up into the grand design which is the work of Redemption. And within that work, there is a crucial drama to be acted out in the new land. But we must be very clear that for Edwards that is a spiritual drama—nothing more, nor less, nor other.

Heimert observes that for Edwards historical events were "subsumed in the grander tale of the spiritual transformation of mankind."[76] And rightly so. Edwards' concern is to affirm the spiritual unity of the race. And this stands behind such texts as these:

God's work of providence, like that of creation, is but one. The events of providence are not so many distinct, independent works; but rather so many different parts of one work, one regular scheme.[77]

God's providence may not unfitly be compared to a river, having innumerable branches, beginning in different regions, and at a great distance one from another, and all conspiring to one common issue. After their very diverse and apparently contrary courses, they all collect together, the nearer they come to their common end, and at length discharge themselves at one mouth into the same ocean. The different streams of this river are apt to appear confused to us, because of our limited sight whereby we cannot see the whole at once. A man who sees but one or two streams at a time, cannot tell what their course tends to. Their course seems very crooked, and different streams seem to run for awhile different and contrary ways; but if we view things at a distance, there seem to be innumerable obstacles and impediments, as rocks, mountains, and the like, in the way of their ever uniting and coming to the ocean; but yet if we trace them, they all unite at last, disgorging themselves in one into the same great ocean. Not one of all the streams fail.[78]

The metaphor is powerful, but dangerous outside its proper context, namely, the work of Redemption. It is this danger which Heimert courts when he subsequently asserts that the "revival and evangelical impulse pressed to a goal of a more beautiful social order— which meant, in the New World, a union of Americans."[79] Such a prospect is outside the purview of Edwards; but it is a danger which Edwards' eschatology courts at this juncture.

When we turn to *Some Thoughts*, published in 1742, we find Edwards on the razor's edge which separates idolatry from discipleship. Against the background of Edwards' metahistorical vision, the events of 1739 through 1741 are read. The title of part 1 of the treatise indicates his intention: "Showing That the Extraordinary Work That Has Of Late Been Going On In This Land, Is a Glorious Work of God."[80] Misjudgment of these events is, argues Edwards, grounded in (1) judging the work a priori, (2) not taking the Scriptures as a whole rule, and (3) not justly separating and distinguishing the good from the bad.[81] The crux of his argument involves a reading of "the times." As he writes, in discussing some biblical texts, "And we live in those latter days, wherein we may be especially warranted to expect that things will be accomplished, concerning which it will be said, 'Who has heard such a thing? Who hath seen such things?' "[82] Lest sheer novelty be the criterion of their divine source, Edwards goes on to say, "And besides, these things in this work that have been chiefly complained of as new, are not so new as has been generally imagined . . . they are not new in their kind; but are things of the same nature as have been found and well approved of in the church of God before, from time to time."[83] And later, "A great deal of noise and tumult, confusion and uproar, and darkness mixed with light, and evil with good, is always to be expected in the beginning of something very extraordinary, and very glorious in the state of things in human society, or the church of God."[84]

That Edwards was predisposed to an eschatological interpretation of the wildfire sweeping through colonial society is clear from our analysis of the *Work of Redemption*. Unlike the opposers of the

Great Awakening, Edwards took his cue from a beckoning future suspended and sustained by the hand of Providence. In his cautious way, Edwards writes:

> If God intends this great revival of religion to be the dawning, or a forerunner of a happy state of his church on earth, it may be an instance of the divine wisdom, in the beginning of it, to suffer so many irregularities and errors in conduct, to which he knew men, in their present weak state, were most exposed, under great religious affections and when animated with great zeal. For it will be very likely to be of excellent benefit to his church, in the continuance and progress of the work afterwards: their experience in the first setting out of the mischievous consequences of these errors, and smarting from them in the beginning, may be an happy defense to them afterwards, for many generations, from these errors, which otherwise they might continually be exposed to.[85]

But even if these considerations are not persuasive, Edwards has another line of defense. He writes: "The visible fruit that is to be expected of a pouring out of the Spirit of God on a country, is a visible reformation in that country. What reformation has lately been brought to pass in New England by this work, has been before observed; and has it not continued long enough already, to give reasonable satisfaction?"[86] His rhetorical question he answers in the affirmative by citing both the extent and numbers who have "been turned from sin to God,"[87] as well as the "alteration in some towns."[88] The evidence is sufficiently overwhelming that Edwards is bold to conclude: "The New Jerusalem in this respect (the extraordinary degree of light, love and spiritual joy) has begun to come down from heaven, and perhaps never were more of the prelibations of heavens glory given upon earth."[89]

The Great Awakening is filled, Edwards acknowledges, with a "great many errors and sinful irregularities."[90] But they are not sufficiently to restrain Edwards from linking these events to the eschatological hope of a dawning millennium. He writes:

> 'Tis not unlikely that this work of God's Spirit, that is so extraordinary and wonderful, is the dawning, or at least a prelude, of that glorious work of God, so often foretold in Scripture, which in the progress and issue of it, shall renew the world of mankind. If we consider how long since the things foretold, as what should precede this great event, have been accomplished; and how long this event has

been expected by the church of God, and thought to be nigh by the
most eminent men of God in the church; and withal consider what
the state of things now is, and has for a considerable time been, in
the church of God and world of mankind, we can't reasonably think
otherwise, than that the beginning of this great work of God must
be near. And there are many things that make it probable that this
work will begin in America.[91]

In comparison to some of his contemporaries, Edwards' comments
are restrained.[92] Nonetheless, it is in relation to such texts that
Goen, for example, argues that Edwards began to "entertain the
idea that God might have purposed to realize the biblical prophecies
in America as a land destined to accomplish the renovation of the
world."[93] Or, as Heimert writes, such affirmations are what led to
the transformation of "the vision of the Work of Redemption . . .
into an ideal of continental union."[94] Such conclusions are unwarranted. Firstly, to describe America as "a land destined to
accomplish the renovation of the world," runs counter to Edwards'
own words. For Edwards, America (meaning simply this land)
might well be the *scene* of the beginning of the millennium, but that
is something very different from suggesting that America (meaning
the Republic, or some kind of active subject) might *accomplish*
the renovation of the world. Secondly, to move as Heimert does
from an eschatological vision to a political goal rests on a confusion
of theology and ideology. Edwards is careful to specify that his
hope for the "new world" is spiritual. As he writes: "This new
world is probably now discovered, that the new and most glorious
state of God's church on earth might commence there; that God
might in it begin a new world in a spiritual respect, when he creates
the new heavens and new earth."[95] Nevertheless, Edwards' does
court the worst of spiritual sins, pride, in these texts. And even
more so when he goes on to say: "And if we may suppose that this
glorious work of God shall begin in any part of America, I think,
if we consider the circumstance of the settlement of New England,
it must needs appear the most likely of all American colonies, to be
the place whence this work shall properly take its rise."[96]

Later Edwards shall have cause to regret these statements. But
here the import of his belief in a dawning new age populated by
the newly converted is significant in relation to its impact on colonial
society. The bulk of *Some Thoughts* is a programmatic statement of

what the various members of society are to do to support this dawning spiritual transformation. Thus it is that in pursuit of the elusive Spirit which is the foundation of this "glorious work of God," Edwards tacitly supports the opening and re-formation of fundamental social questions. The intertwining of the spiritual and societal is abundantly clear when Edwards' work is compared to that of the leader of the antirevival forces, Charles Chauncy, in *Seasonable Thoughts on the State of Religion in New England*.[97] Published in 1743, *Seasonable Thoughts* is an eloquent plea against the revival as unleashing forces which would destroy the good order of society.

The radical consequences of the millennial impulse are particularly manifest in relation to the questions of itinerant preaching and stations or offices. Chauncy is particularly disturbed by the social uproar generated by the Awakening. The foundation of Chauncy's critique is the belief that "Good Order is the Strength and Beauty of the World."[98] It is upon good order that "the prosperity of both Church and State depends."[99] And such order is threatened "where men transgress the limits of their station and intermeddle in the business of others."[100] Chauncy's outrage at the social effects of the Awakening is scarcely masked when he writes, "women and girls; yea, Negros, have taken upon them to do the business of preachers and people must stay in their place, follow their calling."[101] The first, and worst, of the "bad things" of the present disorder is itinerant preaching, to which Chauncy devotes more than 150 pages, followed by the "regard to impulses and impressions," "not following one's calling," "screaming and shrieking in church," and a "spirit of error."[102]

When the Awakening called into question the role of the clergy and challenged the fixedness of stations, the whole authority structure of pre-1740 society was shaken. For Edwards, these were not intended but incidental consequences of this "glorious work." Chauncy was not opposed to the "workings of the Spirit"; it is just that he gave his allegiance to a very different spirit—one that would not generate such turmoil! For Chauncy, "when Men are effectually wrought upon by divine Grace, the roughness of their temper shall be smoothed, their passions restrained and brought into order, so that they shall live together in Love and Peace, doing to each other all the offices, not only of Humanity, but of Christian

Kindness and Charity."[103] In a word, "this Change in Men would make them mild and gentle."[104] The Spirit does not, argues Chauncy, so transform men, that the good order of society is threatened. Rather, the Spirit that Chauncy affirmed strengthened society by confirming men and women in the exercise of their "states, relations, and conditions."[105] The fruits of the Spirit are standard: love, joy, peace, long suffering, gentleness, etc.[106] But the explication of these tells the real story. For example "peace," for Chauncy "meant, not so much a holy serenity of Mind, . . . as that state of outward Quietness, and good Order."[107] Thus, religion was placed in the service of the maintenance of the present order. As Chauncy says, "the End of the Influence of the *Spirit* of GOD . . . 'tis to fit their [men's] Powers for religious Exercise, and preserve them in a State of due Subordination."[108]

Chauncy is neither "asham'd or afraid" to suggest that the power of the magistrate be used to restrain the Awakeners and the Awakened.[109] That is not surprising since what is threatened, in Chauncy's judgment, is the whole of civilization. Chauncy pleads for restraint, sobriety, orderliness, prudence and dutiful exercise of one's station. That plea is not rooted in self-interest only, but also in Chauncy's belief in the mode of God's divine governance. The Creator establishes the orderliness of the world, Christ redeems mankind, and the Spirit confirms and assists men and women in the exercise of their ecclesiastically defined station. But when preachers took to the road and the Awakened claimed a "new birth" which took priority over their station, this order shuddered and crumbled.

Edwards did not so much promote, or even affirm, these social consequences as allow them to stand as the side effects of a dawning new age. In *Some Thoughts* he was concerned to modify or correct excess, but within the overall context of affirmation. Moreover, within the context of his congregation he sought to channel the new energies into social forms which would build up civil society. In March 1742, Edwards led his people into a public renewal of their "covenant with God"[110] which included the following:

> In the management of public affairs . . . we will not make our own worldly gain, or honor, or interest in the affections of others, or getting the better of any of a contrary party, that are in any respect our competitors, or the bringing or keeping them down, our govern-

ing aim, to the prejudice of the interest of religion and the honor of Christ.

And in the management of any public affair wherein there is a difference of opinions, concerning any outward possessions, privileges, rights or properties: we will not wittingly violate justice for private interest.[111]

But in all of this, Edwards' eye was directed towards the spiritual transformation of the people: a transformation he saw exceeding his fondest hopes in the events of 1739–41.

Edwards' eschatology thus contributed to a revolutionary critique of the social order, a critique which left post-Awakening society scrambling on a different terrain. The powerful millennial belief served to undergird the fundamental questioning of the nature of authority and the role of the ordinary man in society. As a child of that tradition which held things spiritual and social in tension, Edwards articulated a metahistorical vision which could reforge the energies of societal life. But he was careful—as careful as one could be given the explosive and unpredictable character of the millennial idiom—to affirm, time and again, the fundamentally spiritual substance of his vision, and thus to warn his hearers of the dangers of transforming its promise into a sanction for their social efforts.

Whether his hearers attended to this critical distinction is doubtful. But we must do Edwards the justice of allowing him to speak in his own voice. When Edwards is heard as articulating an American vocation that finds its fulfillment in the Republic we have not heard him aright. Though he is willing to affirm for America a place within the divine work of Redemption, Edwards overspeaks the question of the Republic.

II. *Eschatology as a Principle of Criticism of Revolutionary Criticism*

By 1742 the dark clouds which had menaced the Great Awakening had gathered and let forth a deluge in the Davenport debacle. In the spring of 1742, Davenport was arrested in Connecticut for violating laws against vagrant preaching. Tried in Hartford, the court judged him "disturbed in the rational faculties of his mind."[112] Davenport retaliated by denouncing the clergy as "unconverted."

And the following March, Davenport led his followers in New London, Connecticut, in burning their "wigs, fine clothes, jewelry, and dangerous books."[113] The demons of fanaticism had been unleashed.

In a letter of May 12, 1743 to the Scottish pastor, James Robe, Edwards sadly wrote: "Now we have not such joyful news to send you; the clouds have lately thickened and our hemisphere is now much darkened with them. There is a great decay of the work of God amongst us, especially as to the awakening and converting influence of the Spirit of God."[114] And on the same day, to another Scottish correspondent, William McCulloch, Edwards wrote: "But God is now going and returning to his place, till we acknowledge our offense, and I hope to humble his Church in New England, and purify it, and so fit it for yet greater comfort, that he designs in due time to bestow upon it."[115] Thus Edwards acknowledged that the late and glorious work was over. And more significantly, he took upon himself the task of humbling and purifying the Church in New England. The incredible self-criticism implicit in these words must be underscored, for Edwards was complicit in the creation of this offense. He had encouraged, however cautiously, the spiritual pride implicit in the belief that the Great Awakening was the dawning of the millennium.

While acknowledging that Edwards "eventually confessed his conclusion [concerning the dawning millennium] to have been not only premature, but inopportune," Heimert nonetheless claims that Edwards continued to "affirm the revivals of 1740–41 to have been 'forerunners' of the millennium."[116] And in another place, Heimert argues that subsequent writings of Edwards "sustained several American generations in a belief that the millennium was not a mere possibility but an imminent and attainable reality."[117] While it is true in a formal sense that Edwards maintained his belief that the Awakening was a "forerunner," that formal affirmation obscures the substantive shift in Edwards' writings after 1742. The intent of Edwards' later eschatological writings was not to sustain a millennial belief, but to criticize the very consequences of the Awakening, consequences that were an "offense."

The first signal of this shift in Edwards is found in his treatise on the *Religious Affections*.[118] Published in 1746, the *Religious Affec-*

tions is still preoccupied by the difficulties spawned by the Great Awakening. As he writes in his preface:

> 'Tis a hard thing to be a hearty zealous friend of what has been *good* and glorious, in the late extraordinary appearances, and to rejoice much in it; and at the same time, to see the evil and pernicious tendency of what has been *bad*, and earnestly to oppose that. But yet, I am humbly, but fully persuaded, we shall never be in the way of truth, nor go on in a way acceptable to God, and tending to the advancement of Christ's kingdom, till we do so.[119]

Although speaking as a defender of the Great Awakening, the scales of "good" and "bad" have shifted; almost two-thirds of the treatise is devoted to a critique of the "pernicious." That New England now found itself in a new situation, Edwards states explicitly in the *Religious Affections* when he attacks pride, personified in the devil, for having "suddenly prevailed to deprive us of the fair prospect, we had a little while ago, of a kind of paradisaic state of the church of God in New England."[120]

The *Religious Affections* is a masterful theological anthropology having, in the words of John Smith, "the central task of defining the soul's relation to God."[121] Edwards' critical distance from the Awakening is underlined when Smith writes concerning its central doctrine that "the true saints have the sense of the heart, a steady and abiding principle in their own natures; something not to be confused with the spectacular emotions and commotions of revivalism."[122]

The first task of overcoming the "offense" is a deepened understanding of the nature of true religion. For Edwards, that consists primarily in "holy affections."[123] An affection is a determinative disposition towards the whole of reality. And here Edwards distinguishes two: love and fear. "There are," says Edwards, "no other principles which human nature is under the influence of that will ever make men conscientious, but one of these two, fear or love."[124] Out of this determinate affection springs the whole of one's being. The ground of holy affections is a supernatural or spiritual reality, the indwelling of the Spirit. Writes Edwards, "Christians are called spiritual persons, because they are born of the Spirit, and because of the indwelling and holy influences of the Spirit of God in them."[125]

Or, later, "The spirit of God is given to the true saints to dwell in them, as his proper and lasting abode; and to influence their hearts, as a principle of new nature, or as a supernatural spring of life and action."[126] The consequence of this indwelling Spirit is a truly "new man." As Edwards writes:

> They that are truly converted are new men, new creatures; new, not only within, but without; they are sanctified throughout, in spirit, soul and body; old things are passed away, all things are become new, they have new hearts, and new eyes, new ears, new tongues, new hands, new feet; i.e., a new conversation and practice; and they walk in newness of life, and continue to do so to the end of life.[127]

Such creatures were not immediately at hand and this does not describe the population of post-Awakening America. The critical impact of these words vis-à-vis the pretension of a society which may, though I doubt it, have confused itself with the dawning millennium is obvious.

It is this dimension—the critical dimension—of Edwards' work that Heimert misses when he writes that the *Religious Affections* "was an exhortation to Edwards' readers to be up and doing, and to the ministers of the colonies to urge their people on their way."[128] Hardly. Rather, we are here encountering an Edwards who has turned his considerable critical powers against the tendency to pride which had been spawned during the Great Awakening. Edwards is here once again honed in on his proper end, which is, in the words which conclude the *Religious Affections*, "to glorify [the] Father which is in heaven."[129]

The substantive shift in Edwards' work from advocate of a dawning millennium to humbler of the Church in New England is further evidenced by the mounting crisis in his own Northampton congregation. Edwards sought to reverse the Half-Way Covenant instituted by his grandfather, Solomon Stoddard, and restrict communion to the "visible saints." This attempt to refashion ecclesiastical polity Heimert ascribes to "the curious workings of his prophetic mind."[130] If, however, we understand the "prophetic mind" as watchfulness in reading "the times," then Edwards' stance is not so curious. According to Edwards, these were times in the "wilderness" where "God will show us our errors, and teach us wisdom by his present withdrawings."[131] What is at stake here, writes Heimart, is Edwards' judgment "of the traditional New England notion of its special covenant with God."[132] The idea of a special New England Covenant is at odds with Edwards' eschatological vision of the Church as "all of one kindred . . . they have a relation to other Christians which they have not to the rest of the world; being of a distinct race from them, but of the same race with one another."[133] Here Edwards uses eschatological materials as the basis of a critique of the present, supposedly more blessed, state of things in America.

The upshot of this controversy was Edwards' dismissal in 1750 from the parish he had served since 1726. Thus if Edwards was the prophet of post-Awakening America, he had been rejected by his own children.

In the midst of these events, Edwards made one last attempt to preserve what he considered to be a legitimate expression of the hope for the coming kingdom. The title of his treatise explains his intent: *A Humble Attempt to Promote Explicit Agreement and Visible Union of God's People in Extraordinary Prayer, For the Revival of Religion and the Advancement of Christ's Kingdom on Earth, Pursuant to Scripture Promises and Prophecies Concerning the Last Time.*[134] The proposal had been initiated in Scotland in 1744, and requested that time be set aside on Saturday evening, Sabbath morning and the first Tuesday of each fourth month.[135] Edwards quoted his Scottish correspondents in citing its purpose:

> *united, extraordinary* applications to the God of all grace, suitably acknowledging Him as the fountain of all the spiritual benefits and blessings of his church, and earnestly praying to Him, that he would *appear in his glory*, and favor Zion, and manifest his compassion to the world of mankind, by an abundant effusion of his Holy Spirit on all the churches, and the whole habitable earth, to revive true religion in all parts of Christendom, and to deliver *all nations* from their great and manifold spiritual calamities and miseries, and bless them with unspeakable benefits of the kingdom of our glorious Redeemer, and *fill the whole earth with his glory.*[136]

To claim, in relation to this proposal, as Heimert does, that this meant "in the New World, a union of Americans,"[137] is simply untenable. Edwards' vision is clearly fixed on a transcendent goal, not an earthly kingdom. And it is the Church which is to bear witness to this transcendent hope. Writes Edwards:

> It is the glory of the Church of Christ, that she in all her members, however dispersed, is thus one holy society, one city, one family, one body; so it is very desirable, that this union should be manifested, and become visible; and so that her distant members should act as one, in those things that concern the common interest of the whole body, in those duties and exercises wherein they have to do with their common Lord and head, as seeking of him the common prosperity.[138]

This is a far cry from the parochialism of Edwards' earlier millennial expectations. And not even within shouting distance of the idolatrous contentions of Heimert.

Nonetheless, the kingdom of God remains for Edwards the end of human longing and striving. As he writes in commenting on the last petition of the Lord's Prayer, "For Thine is the kingdom, and the power, and the glory for ever. Amen," these

> words imply a request that God would take to himself his great power and reign, and manifest his power and glory in the world. Thus Christ teaches us that it becomes his disciples to seek this above all other things, and to make it the first and last in their prayers, and that every petition should be put up in a subordination to the advancement of God's kingdom and glory in the world.[139]

And lest this be taken as a divine sanction for human activity rather than a prayer for supernatural assistance, Edwards writes, after surveying the present state of world history:

> There is much in the present state of things to show us our great need of his mercy, and to cause us to desire it; so there is much to convince us that God alone can bestow it, and show us our entire and absolute dependence on him for it. The insufficiency of human abilities to bring to pass any such happy change in the world as is foretold, or to afford any remedy to mankind from such miseries as have been mentioned, does now remarkably appear.[140]

Though Edwards did not succeed in humbling the Church in New England, his own humbling is here nearly complete. The eschatological vision regains its proper end, namely, God himself who is also its proper agent. Moreover, the eschatological vision retains its power to undergird the life of faith amidst the vagaries of historical time. Edwards gives expression to this faith in these words:

> And thus it is meet, that the last kingdom which shall take place on earth, should be the kingdom of God's own Son and heir, whose right it is to rule and reign; and whatever revolutions and confusions there may be in the world, for a long time, the cause of truth, the righteous cause, should finally prevail, and God's holy people should at last inherit the earth, and reign on earth; and that the world should continue in tumults and great revolutions, following one another, from age to age, the world being as it were in travail, until truth and holiness are brought forth, that all things should be shaken, until that comes which is true and right, and agreeable to the mind of God, which cannot be shaken; and that the wisdom of the Ruler of the world should be manifested in the bringing all things ultimately to so good an issue. The world is made for the Son of God; his kingdom is the end of all changes, that come to pass in the state of the world of mankind; all are only to prepare the way for this; it is fit therefore that the last kingdom on earth should be his.[141]

Our reading of Edwards requires that we acknowledge a discontinuity between his pre- and post-1742 writings: a discontinuity aimed at expunging the spiritual pride engendered by the expectation of a dawning millennium. This runs counter to Heimert's reading which continually suggests that Edwards' vision is being fulfilled in post-Awakening American history. He quotes with approval Edwards' observation that "union is not only beautiful, but profitable too."[142] And he goes on to say that "The revival and the evangelical impulse pressed to the goal of a more beautiful social order—which meant, in the New World, a union of Americans, freed from the covenant relationships of the parochial past and united by the love which God's American children bore for one another."[143] But Edwards' whole quote reads: "Such a union in prayer for the general outpouring of the Spirit of God, would not only be beautiful, but profitable too. It would tend very much to promote union and charity between distant members of the church of Christ, and a public spirit, and love to the Church of God, and concern for the interest of Zion."[144] Perhaps Heimert's reading is consistent with Americolatry, but Edwards' concern was a union in

prayer as an expression of the universality of the church in relation
to its eschatological end.

Formally, the proposal did not come to fruition, though it continued to be read and to inspire many for generations. More significantly from our point of view, it can be read as Edwards' last
attempt to give a public form to Christian eschatological hope. In
Edwards' other major work from this period, his *Memoirs of the
Rev. David Brainerd*, the concern for "the advancement and en-
largement of the kingdom of Christ in the World"[145] is articulated
in terms of the solitary saint.

David Brainerd, who died in Edwards' Northampton home in
1747 at age thirty, was a missionary to the Indians. Edwards edited
his diaries for publication and included a chapter of "Reflections on
the preceding Memoirs."[146] In the preface Edwards explains his
intention in publishing the life: to recommend "true religion" by
way of "example."[147] In his "Reflections," Edwards reminds his
readers that true religion is grounded in God Himself rather than
self-interest or any partial good. He writes:

> Brainerd's religion was not *selfish* and *mercenary*; his love to God
> was primarily and principally for the supreme excellency of his *own
> nature*, and not built on a preconceived notion that God loved *him*,
> had received *him* into favor, and had done great things *for him*, or
> promised great things *to him*. His joy was joy in *God*, and not in
> *himself*.[148]

Thus Edwards sought to free religion from even the most subtle
vestiges of narcissism; something he had fought against on a societal
level he now scourged from personal piety as well.

Not surprisingly, Heimert interprets the *Memoirs* as laying the
ground for that well-known American virtue: activism. Subsequent
to its publication, writes Heimert, "likeness to God became for
evangelical America a state not of being but of doing."[149] And not
only doing, but *pleasurable* doing for, according to Heimert, Edwards "sought largely to convey the pleasures experienced by the
saint in a life of virtuous activity."[150] Such hardly seems to be the
thrust behind Edwards' description of Brainerd's practice: "He
[Brainerd] took up and embraced the *cross* and bore it constantly,
in his great self-denials, labors, and sufferings for the name of
Jesus, and went on without fainting, without repining, to his dying

illness."[151] Rather, Edwards portrays the life of the saint as solitary
and difficult, though finally sustained not by

> any thoughts concerning his own distinguished happy and exalted
> circumstances, as a high favorite of Heaven: but the sweet medi-
> tations and refreshing views he had of divine things *without himself*;
> the affecting considerations and lively ideas of God's infinite glory,
> his unchangeable blessedness, his sovereignty and universal dominion;
> together with the sweet exercises of love to God, giving himself up
> to him, abasing himself before him, denying himself for him, de-
> pending upon him, acting for his glory, diligently serving him; and
> the pleasing prospects or hopes he had of a future advancement of
> the Kingdom of Christ.[152]

The center of this piety was "Holiness, conformity to God, living
to God, and glorifying him."[153] And fidelity to this center was sufficient unto itself. That this was not the dominant piety of "Awakened" America, Edwards states explicitly. Brainerd was "an extraordinary, and almost unparalleled instance in these times, and
these parts of the world."[154] It was a piety, writes Edwards, which
led Brainerd

> from time to time [to] relinquish and renounce the *world* secretly in
> his heart, with the full and fervent consent of all the powers of his
> soul . . . [and to] openly and actually forsake the *world* with its pos-
> sessions, delights, and common comforts, to dwell as it were with
> wild beasts, in a howling wilderness; with constant cheerfulness,
> complying with numerous hardships of a life of toil and travail there,
> to promote the kingdom of his dear Redeemer.[155]

These words were not only a description of Brainerd, but a self
prophecy as well. Edwards, who helped give birth to millennial
America and was rejected by his own congregation in the process
of attempting to purify the New England church, went off into the
wilderness. Secure only in the knowledge that the life of faith was
"to glorify God and enjoy him forever," he left millennial America.

III. *Eschatology as a Principle of Transtemporal Criticism*

We have argued for a substantive development of Edwards'
eschatology such that we have an Edwards I and II. Beyond this
we would argue that there is a third stage of development—
Edwards III. The primary evidence for this third Edwards is to be

found in the post-1750 writings: the *Dissertation Concerning the End for Which God Created the World, The Nature of True Virtue, The Great Christian Doctrine of Original Sin Defended,* and *A Careful and Strict Inquiry Into the Modern Prevailing Notions of the Freedom of the Will.* Since a full analysis of these major works obviously exceeds the scope of our intention here, a sketch of the main lines of the arguments must suffice.

If the dominant symbolic universe of the American tradition is centered in affirmations of an undetermined will, innocence and this-worldliess, then his post-1750 writings clearly place Edwards outside that tradition. Indeed, Edwards' works on the will, original sin, virtue, and the end of creation can be seen as among the earliest examples of an intellectual criticism directed against dimensions of that symbolic universe which, having its roots in the Awakening, came to form the American tradition. The absence of millennial reflections is conspicuous in these works, indicating that Edwards is here moving on a new terrain.

The failure of interpreters such as Heimert to allow for significant shifts in Edwards' thinking results in these works being claimed to support the emergence of *the* American tradition. In Heimert's configuration, the *Freedom of the Will* becomes a "source of historical optimism," for it allowed "pious Americans . . . to exert themselves on behalf of what was thought to be the ordained destiny of God's people."[156] *Original Sin* becomes significant for a conception of "natural man" which was "the central truth" of Calvinist politics.[157] The *Nature of True Virtue* reveals "in substance" that God was for Edwards "a supremely excellent Christian Commonwealth."[158] And the *Dissertation* becomes one of the works which "sustained several American generations in a belief that the millenium was not a mere possibility but an imminent and attainable reality."[159] Nowhere does Heimert allow that Edwards might have cared less about the course of contemporary events, especially politics, and that his preoccupation was with a realm that transcended every historical era, having its center in the eternal life of the Trinity. In a word, that Edwards was truly a theologian, and not an ideologist in pious dress.

The *Freedom of the Will* was written against the "Arminian" (a title Edwards uses for convenience[160]) notion of the will as "self-

determining."[161] The Arminian "scheme" was something Edwards
had long opposed, beginning with the revivals of 1734–35. Goen
acknowledges the difficulty of specifying precisely Edwards' early
opponents and argues that Edwards was concerned to counter " a
mood of rising confidence in man's ability to gain some purchase
on the divine favor by human endeavor."[162] By 1754, this mood
was much more widespread.

Edwards rejects the notion of a self-determining will as absurd,
yet painstakingly goes through all the arguments. Affirming that
"the soul always wills or chooses that which, in the present view of
the mind, considered in the whole of that view, and all that belongs
to it, appears most agreeable,"[163] Edwards is committed to an
understanding of the will as determined. In an eloquent metaphor,
Edwards writes, "the whole state of the world of mankind, in all
ages, and the very being of every person who has ever lived in it, in
every age, since the times of the ancient prophets, has depended
on more volitions, or acts of the wills of men, than there are sands
on the seashore.[164] The thrust of Edwards' argument is to set the
will within the context of ongoing history, and, thereby, affirm the
unity and interrelatedness of the human drama.

The principle of universality is likewise central to Edwards' work
on *Original Sin*. Published posthumously, Edwards focuses on the
unity of the race in sin, a reality which has its source not in the
furnishings of the world but in the nature of man. This tendency to
sin, writes Edwards, "is *inherent*, and is seated in that nature which
is common to all mankind, which they carry with them wherever
they go, and still remains the same, however circumstances may
differ."[165] Such is cold comfort to an Awakened society which may
have entertained a more exalted view of themselves. But Edwards
is relentless and continues:

> In God's sight no man living can be justified; but all are sinners, and
> exposed to condemnation. This is true of persons of all constitutions,
> capacities, conditions, manners, opinions and education; in all
> countries, climates, nations, and ages; and through all the mighty
> changes and revolutions, which have come to pass in the habitable
> world.[166]

Need we say that this includes millennial America?[167]

Taken together, *Freedom of the Will* and *Original Sin*, exhibit Edwards doing theology against a backdrop of the unity of mankind in sin and redemption. Such a context is undergirded by a doctrine of divine Providence as the transtemporal vantage point for viewing the human drama.

The *Nature of True Virtue*, a philosophical counterpart to the *Dissertation*, elaborates Edwards' ethical views. The foundation of his position is the assertion that "true virtue most essentially consists in *benevolence to being in general*."[168] This affectional disposition may be the ground of "exercises of love to particular beings, as objects are presented and occasions arise."[169] But the crucial point is that "affection to a private society or system, independent of general benevolence, cannot be of the nature of true virtue."[170] The critical impact of this analysis is to undercut any partial thing, no matter how noble, as the ground of true virtue. Or, in less formal terms, even the millennium *itself* is not being-in-general! True virtue has an even deeper ground. In theological terms, "true virtue does primarily and most essentially consist in a supreme love to God; and that where this is wanting, there can be no true virtue."[171]

It follows from this definition of true virtue, that "all sin has its source from selfishness, or from self-love not subordinate to a regard to being in general."[172] That Edwards is aware of the social consequences of his view is obvious when he writes:

> For the reasons which have been given, it is undeniably true, that if persons have a benevolent affection limited to a party, or to the nation in general of which they are a part, or the public community to which they belong, though it be as large as the Roman Empire was of old . . . exclusive of union of heart to general existence and love to God . . . it cannot be of the nature of true virtue.[173]

Such an ethic undercuts a notion of virtue grounded in any particular nation, people or land, *even if that nation be a millennial creation*.

The *Dissertation Concerning the End for Which God Created the World* is a complex argument and a litany on a single theme: the end of creation is *the glory of God*.[174] The "ultimate" as well as "great and last" end is the "glory of God."[175] Lest there be any doubt that God is His own end, Edwards writes, "The notion of

God's creating the world in order to receive any thing properly from the creature, is not only contrary to the nature of God, but inconsistent with the notion of creation."[176] When Edwards writes that "it is a thing infinitely good in itself that God's glory should be known by a glorious society of created beings,"[177] it is not to underwrite a political venture, but to indicate the purpose of the Church.

The creation is consequent upon God's inclination "to communicate of his infinite fulness."[178] Or, "God's seeking himself in the creation of the world is" writes Edwards, consequent upon "a delight in his own internal fulness and glory," which "disposes him to an abundant effusion and emanation of that glory."[179] If such an understanding of creation has any relevance to sociocultural life, it is to undercut any belief that God underwrites any human venture whatsoever. It is God Himself who is the end of creation—not any earthly creation.

It is, of course, crucial that the creature should know the end, for it is the distinction of intelligent creatures of "actively complying with his design in their creation and promoting it."[180] The end of all creation is transhistorical and spiritual: the glory of God. Edwards concludes his dissertation with two crucial texts:

(1) It is no solid objection against God's aiming at an infinitely perfect union of the creature with himself, that the particular time will never come when it can be said, the union is now infinitely perfect.[181]

(2) God, in glorifying the saints in heaven with eternal felicity, aims to satisfy his infinite grace or benevolence, by the bestowment of a good infinitely valuable, because eternal; and yet there will never come the moment, when it can be said, that now this infinitely valuable good has been actually bestowed.[182]

The distinction implicit in these texts is the old Augustinian distinction of two ends of man, one natural and the other supernatural. The supernatural end of man attains its fulfillment "in heaven" which is an eternal, transtemporal realm. Not only is Edwards affirming that the union of the creature with the Creator is inaugurated historically to gain its fulfillment beyond history, but also that even in eternity that union is deepened. Similarly, the communion of saints does not have an historical termination but an eternal one. Here, it appears, Edwards has altogether forsaken an eschatology which would see the historical process terminating in any this-worldly kingdom of God—no matter how perfect. Moreover, like Augustine, Edwards also argues that the saved and the damned are forever mixed historically and await the Last Judgment for their final separation.

Although there are grounds to warrant our claim for an Augustinian development in Edwards' thought, its full textual confirmation is cut off by Edwards' death in 1758. However, the sources available do reveal an Edwards who is moving in the realm proper to theological investigation, namely, the realm of God himself. Such theological work is at least two steps removed from the Edwards who, albeit with caution, encouraged the Awakened of the early 1740s to believe that the whole cosmic drama might come to its resolution in America. Such millennial tendencies had been expunged from his thinking through an eschatology which now became the principle of criticism of every historical epoch, even, and most difficulty, his own. Thus Edwards grew to be a theologian of the glory of God.

IV. Conclusions

Our investigation now allows us to return to a formulation of the secret of the American tradition. Nourished by the belief in a dawning millennium, a deep strand of America's self-understanding suspects that America is the object of the work of Redemption. Thus, the sociopolitical history subsequent to the Great Awakening, including the events which led to the formation of the Republic, are implicitly nourished by this suspicion. From this perspective, the Republic can be understood as a realization of the millennial hope.

Though Edwards was complicit in this initial confusion of the millennium with America, a careful reading of his work will not allow the American tradition to claim him as tutor. For Edwards, America did have a vocation within the work of Redemption; but America's vocation was spiritual, not political. For Edwards, America was not the Republic. Moreover, Edwards saw the spiritual pride implicit in a "millennial America" and sought to exorcise the demon. That required a humbling which a self-confident, post-Awakening society would not heed. Edwards, however, heeded. He was not immune from the need for humility, and for that he was sent out. Out, beyond America, in the "howling wilderness," Edwards regained his orientation while living with the Indians and learning their language. A similar act of humbling is also today required of America if Edwards is to be its tutor. Only through some such dramatic act can America's Jacob experience be redeemed from the curse it has become.

In more formal terms, the critical question underlying this essay is this: Are the principles and symbols of American social self-transcendence adequate? Is it accidental that the millennial hope is continually immanentized, thus condemning the Republic to oscillate from one political extreme to another? Are the millennial symbols which lie deep in the American tradition inherently inadequate to the societal need for continual self-transcendence and, hence, social transformation?

NOTES

1. John Adams, quoted in A. M. Schlesinger, *New Viewpoints in American History,* (New York: Macmillan, 1922) p. 161, as quoted in Eugen Rosenstock-Huessy, *Out of Revolution: Autobiography of Western Man* (Norwich, Vt.: Argo Books, 1969), p. 644.

2. Nathan Cole, "Conversion: The Spiritual Travels of Nathan Cole, 1741,"*The Great Awakening: Documents on the Revival of Religion,* ed. R. L. Bushman (New York: Atheneum, 1970), p. 68, 70.

3. Cole, p. 70.

4. Among the several sources for this sociocultural definition of the relationship between religion and revolution, in which the transformation of consciousness is the ground of sociocultural transformation, are the following: Eugen Rosenstock-Huessy, *Out of Revolution,* Vittorio Lanternari, *The Religions of the Oppressed: A Study of Modern Messianic Cults* (New York: Mentor Books, 1965) and *Marx and Engels on Religion,* ed. R. Niebuhr (New York: Schocken Books, 1964). This sociocultural understanding presupposes a more sociological definition

of religion as a symbolic constellation which provides the integrating and legitimating bases for social life. See, for example, C. Geertz, "Religion as a Cultural System," *The Religious Situation 1968*, ed. D. Cutler (Boston: Beacon Press, 1969), Robert Bellah, *Beyond Belief: Essays on Religion in a Post-Modern World* (New York: Harper & Row, 1970), P. Berger and T. Luckmann, *The Social Construction of Reality: A Treatise in the Sociology of Knowledge* (Garden City: Doubleday, 1967), as well as the classical works of E. Durkheim and M. Weber.

5. Bernard Bailyn. *The Ideological Origins of the American Revolution* (Cambridge: Harvard University Press, 1967), p. 32.

6. Bailyn, p. 32.

7. Bailyn, p. 33.

8. Bailyn, p. 33.

9. Robert Bellah, see note at beginning of the essay, "Civil Religion in America," *Beyond Belief*, p. 168.

10. Perry Miller, *Errand Into the Wilderness* (New York: Harper & Row, 1964).

11. John Winthrop, quoted in D. B. Rutman, ed., *The Great Awakening: Event and Exegesis* (New York: John Wiley & Sons, 1970), p. 5.

12. M. Darrol Bryant, "Beyond Messianism: Toward a New American Civil Religion," *The Ecumenist* XI, 4 (May–June, 1973), pp. 49–51.

13. Rosenstock-Huessy, pp. 288 ff. See also Michael Walzer, *The Revolution of the Saints: A Study in the Origins of Radical Politics* (New York: Atheneum, 1968) which credits the Puritans with originating the modern notion of political activity as disciplined, sustained, intentional, and ideological activity.

14. C. C. Goen, ed., *Works of Jonathan Edwards: The Great Awakening* (New Haven: Yale University Press, 1972), 4:32.

15. See, for example, the *Oxford History of the United States*.

16. Alan Heimert, *Religion and the American Mind: From the Great Awakening to the Revolution* (Cambridge: Harvard University Press, 1966), p. 59.

17. Perry Miller, "From the Covenant to the Revival," *The Shaping of American Religion*, ed. J. W. Smith and A. L. Jamison (Princeton: Princeton Univ. Press, 1961), 1.

18. Goen, p. 32.

19. Heimert, pp. 98–99.

20. George Bancroft, *History of the United States* (Boston: Little & Brown, 1842), 2:986–987.

21. Perry Miller, *The New England Mind: From Colony to Province* (Boston: Beacon Press, 1953), p. 482.

22. See, for example, R. L. Bushman, *From Puritan to Yankee: Character and the Social Order in Connecticut, 1690–1765* (Cambridge: Harvard University Press, 1967).

23. Miller, *The New England Mind*, p. 484.

24. See Ola Winslow, *Jonathan Edwards 1703–1758: A Biography* (New York: Macmillan, 1940).

25. S. J. Stein, "A Note on the Apocalypse by Jonathan Edwards," *William and Mary Quarterly* 29, 4 (October 1972): 623.

26. Goen, p. 1.

27. Jonathan Edwards, "Five Discourses on Important Subjects Nearly Concerning the Great Affair of the Soul's Eternal Salvation," *Works of President Edwards* (reprints ed., New York: Ben Franklin, 1968), 6:207–432.

28. Jonathan Edwards, "A Faithful Narrative," *The Great Awakening*, ed. C. C. Goen, 4:97–211. All quotations of the *Faithful Narrative* are from this text, hereafter cited as the *Faithful Narrative*.

29. Jonathan Edwards, "Some Thoughts Concerning the Revival," *The Great Awakening*, ed. C. C. Goen, IV, pp. 289–530. All quotations of *Some Thoughts* are from this text, hereafter cited as *Some Thoughts*.

30. Edwards, *Faithful Narrative*, p. 118.

31. Edwards, *Faithful Narrative*, p. 184.

32. Edwards, *Faithful Narrative*, pp. 189–190.

33. Edwards, *Faithful Narrative*, p. 190.

34. Edwards, *Faithful Narrative*, p. 210.

35. Jonathan Edwards, *A History of the Work of Redemption Comprising an Outline of Church History* (New York: The American Tract Society, n.d.).

36. Peter Gay, *A Loss of Mastery: Puritan Historians in Colonial America* (Berkeley: University of California Press, 1966).

37. C. C. Goen, "Jonathan Edwards: A New Departure in Eschatology," *Church History*, XXVIII (1959), pp. 25–41.

38. Goen, "A New Departure," p. 26.

39. Goen, "A New Departure," p. 29.

40. See Northrop Frye, *Anatomy of Criticism* (New York: Atheneum, 1966).

41. See, for example, Mircea Eliade, *The Myth of the Eternal Return*, (New York: Pantheon Books, 1954).

42. Edwards, *Work of Redemption*, p. 17.

43. Edwards, *Work of Redemption*, p. 16.

44. Edwards, *Work of Redemption*, p. 12.
45. Goen, "A New Departure," p. 26.
46. Heimert, *Religion and the American Mind*, p. 99.
47. Edwards, *Work of Redemption*, p. 23.
48. Edwards, *Work of Redemption*, p. 23.
49. Edwards, *Work of Redemption*, p. 21.
50. Edwards, *Work of Redemption*, pp. 21–22.
51. Edwards, *Work of Redemption*, p. 23.
52. Edwards, *Work of Redemption*, p. 24.
53. Edwards, *Work of Redemption*, p. 24.
54. Edwards, *Work of Redemption*, p. 24.
55. Jonathan Edwards, "Miscellaneous Observations on Important Doctrines," *Works of Jonathan Edwards* (New York: Leavitt & Allen, 1843) I, p. 596.
56. Edwards, *Work of Redemption*, p. 438.
57. Heimert, *Religion and the American Mind*, p. 79.
58. Edwards, *Work of Redemption*, p. 436.
59. Edwards, *Some Thoughts*, p. 374.
60. Edwards, *Work of Redemption*, pp. 5–7.
61. Goen, *The Great Awakening*, intro., p. 72.
62. Edwards, *Work of Redemption*, p. 373.
63. Edwards, *Work of Redemption*, p. 373.
64. Edwards, *Work of Redemption*, p. 375.
65. Edwards, *Work of Redemption*, p. 376.
66. Edwards, *Work of Redemption*, p. 378.
67. Edwards, *Work of Redemption*, p. 384.
68. Edwards, *Work of Redemption*, p. 385.
69. Edwards, *Work of Redemption*, p. 386.
70. Edwards, *Work of Redemption*, p. 395.
71. Edwards, *Work of Redemption*, p. 397.
72. Edwards, *Work of Redemption*, p. 399.
73. Edwards, *Works of Redemption*, p. 400.
74. Edwards, *Work of Redemption*, p. 444.
75. Edwards, *Work of Redemption*, p. 439.
76. Heimert, *Religion and the American Mind*, p. 67.
77. Edwards, *Works of Redemption*, p. 435.
78. Edwards, *Work of Redemption*, pp. 435–436.
79. Heimert, *Religion and the American Mind*, p. 95.
80. Edwards, *Some Thoughts*, p. 293.
81. Edwards, *Some Thoughts*, p. 293.
82. Edwards, *Some Thoughts*, p. 307.

83. Edwards, *Some Thoughts*, p. 307.
84. Edwards, *Some Thoughts*, p. 318.
85. Edwards, *Some Thoughts*, pp. 323-324.
86. Edwards, *Some Thoughts*, p. 343.
87. Edwards, *Some Thoughts*, p. 345.
88. Edwards, *Some Thoughts*, p. 346.
89. Edwards, *Some Thoughts*, p. 346.
90. Edwards, *Some Thoughts*, p. 347.
91. Edwards, *Some Thoughts*, p. 353.
92. See, for example, Samuel Finley, "Christ Triumphing and Satan Raging . . . Wherein is Proven, That the Kingdom of God is Come Unto Us This Day," Rutman, ed., pp. 70–79.
93. Goen, "A New Departure," p. 29.
94. Heimert, *Religion and the America Mind*, p. 100.
95. Edwards, *Some Thoughts*, p. 354.
96. Edwards, *Some Thoughts*, p. 358.
97. Charles Chauncy, *Seasonable Thoughts on the State of Religion in New England* (Boston: Rogers & Fowle, 1743).
98. Chauncy, p. 366.
99. Chauncy, p. 366.
100. Chauncy, p. 366.
101. Chauncy, p. 226.
102. Chauncy, pp. 50 ff.
103. Chauncy, p. 16.
104. Chauncy, p. 17.
105. Chauncy, p. 320.
106. Chauncy, pp. 25 ff.
107. Chauncy, p. 28.
108. Chauncy, pp. 327–328.
109. Charles Chauncy, "Seasonable Thoughts on the State of Religion," *The Great Awakening: Documents Illustrating the Crisis and its Consequences*, eds. A. Heimert and P. Miller (New York: Bobbs-Merrill, 1967), pp. 300–301.
110. Jonathan Edwards, from a collection of letters written by Edwards as they appear in *The Great Awakening*, IV, p. 550.
111. Edwards, *Letters*, p. 552.
112. Goen, *The Great Awakening*, intro., p. 60.
113. Goen, *The Great Awakening*, intro., p. 61.
114. Edwards *Letters*, IV, p. 536.
115. Edwards, *Letters*, p. 540.
116. Heimert, *Religion and the American Mind*, p. 62.

117. Heimert, *Religion and the American Mind*, pp. 60–61.

118. Jonathan Edwards, *The Works of Jonathan Edwards: Religious Affections*, ed. John E. Smith (New Haven: Yale University Press, 1959), II, p. 85.

119. Edwards, *Religious Affections*, p. 85.

120. Edwards, *Religious Affections*, p. 87.

121. John E. Smith (ed.), *Religious Affections*, intro., pp. 1, 9.

122. John E. Smith, p. 9.

123. Edwards, *Religious Affections*, p. 95.

124. Edwards, *Religious Affections*, p. 179.

125. Edwards, *Religious Affections*, p. 198.

126. Edwards, *Religious Affections*, p. 200.

127. Edwards, *Religious Affections*, p. 391.

128. Edwards, *Religious Affections*, p. 132.

129. Edwards, *Religious Affections*, p. 461.

130. Heimert, *Religion and the American Mind*, p. 125.

131. Edwards, *Letters*, p. 540.

132. Heimert, *Religion and the American Mind*, p. 126.

133. Heimert, *Religion and the American Mind*, p. 126.

134. Jonathan Edwards, *A Humble Attempt to Promote Explicit Agreement and Visible Union of God's People in Extraordinary Prayer, For the Revival of Religion and the Advancement of Christ's Kingdom on Earth, Pursuant to Scripture Promises and Prophecies Concerning the Last Time*, in *Works of Jonathan Edwards* (Worcester ed.) (New York: Leavitt and Allen, 1844), III, pp. 427–508.

135. Edwards, *A Humble Attempt*, p. 435.

136. Edwards, *A Humble Attempt*, p. 435.

137. Heimert, *Religion and the American Mind*, p. 95.

138. Edwards, *A Humble Attempt*, p. 463.

139. Edwards, *A Humble Attempt*, p. 453.

140. Edwards, *A Humble Attempt*, p. 459.

141. Edwards, *A Humble Attempt*, p. 445.

142. Heimert, *Religion and the American Mind*, p. 95.

143. Heimert, *Religion and the American Mind*, p. 95.

144. Edwards, *A Humble Attempt*, p. 463.

145. Jonathan Edwards, "Memoirs of the Rev. David Brainerd; Missionary to the Indians on the Border of New-York, New-Jersey, and Pennsylvania: Chiefly Taken From His Own Diary," *Memoirs of the Rev. David Brainerd*, ed. Sereno Edwards Dwight (St. Clair Shores, Michigan: Scholarly Press, 1970), p. 460.

146. Edwards, *Memoirs*, p. 432.

147. Edwards, *Memoirs*, p. 29.
148. Edwards, *Memoirs*, p. 437.
149. Heimert, *Religion and the American Mind*, p. 313.
150. Heimert, *Religion and the American Mind*, p. 313.
151. Edwards, *Memoirs*, p. 443.
152. Edwards, *Memoirs*, p. 437.
153. Edwards, *Memoirs*, p. 437.
154. Edwards, *Memoirs*, p. 443.
155. Edwards, *Memoirs*, p. 443.
156. Heimert, *Religion and the American Mind*, p. 313.
157. Heimert, *Religion and the American Mind*, p. 388.
158. Heimert, *Religion and the American Mind*, p. 104.
159. Heimert, *Religion and the American Mind*, pp. 60–61.
160. Jonathan Edwards, *The Works of Jonathan Edwards: Freedom of the Will*, ed. Paul Ramsey (New Haven: Yale University Press, 1957), I, pp. 131–132.
161. Edwards, *Freedom of the Will*, p. 164.
162. Goen, intro. to *The Great Awakening*, p. 10.
163. Edwards, *Freedom of the Will*, p. 217.
164. Edwards, *Freedom of the Will*, p. 250.
165. Jonathan Edwards, *The Works of Jonathan Edwards: Original Sin*, ed. Clyde A. Holbrook (New Haven: University Press, 1970), III, p. 124.
166. Edwards, *Original Sin*, p. 124.
167. One wonders what might have been the course of Jonathan Edwards' theological development (and, by implication, his impact on the American tradition) if this work had inaugurated rather than concluded his theological work.
168. Jonathan Edwards, *The Nature of True Virtue* (Ann Arbor: University of Michigan Press, 1960), p. 3.
169. Edwards, *True Virtue*, p. 5.
170. Edwards, *True Virtue*, p. 21.
171. Edwards, *True Virtue*, p. 18.
172. Edwards, *True Virtue*, p. 92.
173. Edwards, *True Virtue*, pp. 78-79.
174. Jonathan Edwards, "Dissertation Concerning the End for which God Created the World," *Works of President Edwards* (New York: Robert Carter and Bros., 1881, reprint of Worcester ed., II.
175. Edwards, *Dissertation*, pp. 226, 246, 254.
176. Edwards, *Dissertation*, p. 200.
177. Edwards, *Dissertation*, p. 205.

178. Edwards, *Dissertation*, p. 213.
179. Edwards, *Dissertation*, p. 215.
180. Edwards, *Dissertation*, p. 225.
181. Edwards, *Dissertation*, p. 257.
182. Edwards, *Dissertation*, p. 257.

HERBERT W. RICHARDSON

3. What Makes a Society Political?

Introduction by Paul Rigby

Introduction

What makes a society political? In answering this question
Herbert Richardson develops a more specific notion of politics than
is commonly understood. Politics, it is sometimes said, concerns
the process of gaining and exercising power within a society. Or,
according to another definition, politics is essentially concerned
with the problem of sustaining social order and steering social
systems. In terms of these two definitions, it might be said that all
societies are political, for all societies have procedures for wielding
social power and all societies are ordered through human acts.

Richardson argues, however, that politics is something more than
this. Recalling the classical definition of politics as the *distribution*
of power, Richardson proposes that there are two kinds of societies: political and nonpolitical. Both have procedures for exercising social power and producing social order. But political
societies seek to distribute power, or sovereignty, to a plural
number of centers of initiative and are forced, thereafter, to create
a social unity through that process of conflict, negotiation, and
compromise which we call "politics." Nonpolitical societies do not
seek to distribute power to a plural number of centers of initiative,
but tend to rely on a single center of initiative (e.g., a strong president, a dominant party, or a technological elite) to wield power and
to establish social order.

A democratic society, suggests Richardson, is not ipso facto
also a political society. Democratic ideas and institutions may be
used as the means to politicize a society, but they also may be
used as the means to destroy its political character and create a
massified, monolithic state. In America, democratic institutions

have been predominantly a means of politicization. Following the American Revolution, the men who created the fundamental institutions of the United States drew upon the basic ideas of the Enlightenment to create a political society: the ideas of "the rights of man," "authority derived from the people," a "free press," and the "disestablishment of all religion." In Richardson's essay, we see how these and other Enlightenment social inventions have been used to politicize American society.

Richardson's fundamental argument, however, is that *political* society takes precedence over *democratic* society and that democratic/Enlightenment institutions may or may not contribute to politicization. Democratic ideology itself needs to be criticized in the light of higher norms. Sometimes "power to the people" creates new centers of initiative and helps a society become political; but sometimes "power to the people" becomes a method for massifying a society, destroying its internal diversity and attenuating its political character. For example, in Nazi Germany democratic ideology was used as an instrument of totalitarian control, when Hitler sought to mobilize and give voice to the will of "the people." In the United States today, the ability of the President to appeal directly to "the people" by mobilizing the mass media also threatens the institutional diversity on which the political character of American society rests.

In the final section of his essay, Richardson discusses the place of religion in political society and argues that the existence of social pluralism presupposes (and is actually created by) the existence of a plurality of particular churches, whose differing conceptions of the goal of life inhibits society from establishing any particular world view as the official one. The idea behind pluralism, Richardson argues, is that the world possesses no immanent principle of unity. Political society presupposes that the unity of the world ("God") utterly transcends the world. Hence, the faith of a political society is always affirmation of the dimension of transcendence.

The affirmation of transcendence can take either a religious or an antireligious form, argues Richardson. For example, against immanentistic or utopian religions, a political society may affirm its faith in the transcendent through "atheism" (i.e., by denying the truth of immanentist or utopian religious claims). Or, from time to time, the form of a political society's faith in the transcendent may be expressed through particular religions. This latter approach has been more characteristic of America, which has tended to use the symbolisms of Judaism, Catholicism, and Protestantism to express its faith in the absolute transcendence of God over every historical affirmation. (The danger that Judaeo-Christian symbolism will be transformed into an immanental, utopian, and antipolitical form is always present, of course. The existence of this tendency in America has been discussed in M. Darrol Bryant's essay.)

Richardson acknowledges that even in a political society there must be some agreement among its members, but insists that this agreement does not take place in the religious sphere and does not involve the affirmation of common myths, values, or goals. At the present time there is much discussion about the thing that binds Americans together, and there are many who affirm that the unity of our society is expressed through a shared "civil religion." From Richardson's point of view, a civil religion is inconsistent with a truly political society. It involves an immanentalization of the principle of unity and reduces the social plurality. Richardson argues that what holds together a political society is not a "civil religion," but the actual process of politics. It is through this process that the plurality of the society is maintained as it seeks to compromise and adjust its differences for the sake of specific finite goals. The sole presupposition of politics is the willingness of the members of a society to cooperate politically—and this willingness can only exist when a society recognizes that its members do *not* share the basic common values affirmed by a "civil religion."

Richardson's view of politics, therefore, is antiutopian and essentially "realistic." Politics, he concludes, "will not bring salvation, cannot make men happy. Its goal is more modest, but no less essential. Politics allows persons and groups that have differing aspirations to live together in relative peace and to cooperate in limited ways for the sake of specific finite benefits. Whenever politics seeks to be more than this, it must inevitably become far less."

What Makes a Society Political?

The purpose of this essay is to explore the fundamental elements of political society. This involves, first, distinguishing various kinds of values that must be maintained within a political process; second, explaining which institutions embody these values and how these institutions are politically effective; third, arguing that political society generates the new "polyconsciousness" that is its own presupposition; and, fourth, showing why the social differentiation necessary to political society has been produced by Judaism, Catholicism, and Protestantism.

I. *Two Kinds of Values*

Values are not simply the preferences that determine the choices of a society, but values are also the preferences that a society adduces in order to justify the way it makes its choices. There are, therefore, two kinds of values. There are those that determine the future goals and choices of a society, and there are those that determine the way a society organizes itself to decide its goals and pursue them. Values that determine our future goals and ultimate choices are *teleological values*. Values that determine the way we organize society in order to decide and pursue our goals are *procedural, or structural, values*.

For example, two societies might have the same goal and share the same teleological value (they might both value private property and seek to eliminate theft). But they might differ in the way they decided upon this goal and worked to attain it. That is, their procedural values might differ. One society might apply techniques of behavior modification (drugs or conditioning techniques) against

100

the will of the subject. Another might reject this method as violating a fundamental value (freedom) for whose preservation the society itself exists.

The different ways that these two societies were ordered would express differing views of man. Differing views of man are logically antecedent to the existence of societies and are the reasons adduced by them to justify their being organized the way they are. For a society to seek any goal in such a way that it contradicts its own procedural, or structural, values is, therefore, for it to contradict its own reason for existing. The critical principle determining all discussion of the goals of a society is that this discussion be done in such a way that a society does not contradict its own procedural values and their institutionalization.

II. *Two Kinds of Societies*

In terms of procedural values, societies can be distinguished into two types: nonpolitical and political. In a nonpolitical society, government originates and presents itself as acting through a single will, or head. In a political society, government originates and presents itself as acting through a multitude of wills, or heads. Nonpolitical societies are monolithic; political societies are pluralistic.

A society seeks to maintain itself structurally nonpolitical by aiming, insofar as possible, to dissolve the plurality of willings into a single general will which is then symbolized as the will of the leader or the party. (So, for example, in totalitarian states it is symbolically urgent that elections take the form of manifesting almost unanimous agreement.) A political society seeks to maintain itself structurally pluralistic by aiming, insofar as possible, to multiply the number and variety of willings within it, and to compromise the various willings within it through a political process that becomes, symbolically, the "head" of the community. (For this reason, elections in political communities tend to symbolize, in their outcomes, the fact of political disagreement; hence, it does not vitiate the claim of a political government to legitimacy if it holds power by a fractional majority.)

If a nonpolitical society seeks a goal in such a way that it becomes structurally pluralistic, then it destroys itself. If a political society seeks a goal in such a way that it becomes structurally monolithic, then it destroys itself. The problem, then, in planning goals and courses of action for America is the problem of deciding them in such a way that the basic procedural, or structural, values of the society are themselves affirmed in the decision-making process. That is, it is the problem of making decisions politically.

III. *The Importance of Political Society*

Political society is a method of government that respects the integrity and freedom of the plural number of its constituent units (whether persons or groups). It recognizes that to seek any goal, however laudable, at the expense of compromising the dignity of the constituent members of that society is to contradict its purpose for existing. For this reason, political society does not make "rational efficiency" or "social order" into its chief values. Rather, it accepts inefficiency, conflict, and disorder to the extent that these are necessarily tolerated if the integrity and rights of its members are also to be respected.

With respect to rational efficiency and social order, therefore, political societies are frequently inferior to nonpolitical societies. But political societies possess a compensating strength, namely, that since they do not define their existence wholly in terms of teleological values (future goals), they are able to change their goals without changing either the government or the symbols of government. Thus political societies gain something in flexibility by giving up something in efficiency; and in an era of rapid social change political societies may even be more "functional" than nonpolitical societies. However, whether this is the case or not, such a functional criterion could never be the primary justification for their existence. Rather, the primary reason for the existence of a political society is that only such a society allows the dignity of man as an individual to be properly affirmed.

IV. *The Uniqueness of Political Society*

Political and nonpolitical societies are not simply different ways of going about the same thing. They are not simply different ways of organizing society, but they are ways of creating quite different kinds of societies. A political society, by virtue of its respect for a plurality of willings, creates a social grouping that has no analogy with a nonpolitical society, namely, the human community.

A political society aims to be a community. This is why, in a political society, the will of its members cannot be expressed or symbolized as the will of a single person or subgroup. Rather, the will of these members can only be expressed and actualized as a new kind of willing: a *co-willing*, a "one-out-of-many." This "community" of the many is not a mere addition of wills; rather, it is a new kind of will, a political process.

A political process is communal. It is more than the will of all the individuals involved. Therefore, it is synergetic. This is why political societies are culturally creative, for in the synergetic political willing an institution is established through which a group of persons can develop beyond the mere collection of their capacities as individuals. But a political process is not a metaphysical "general will" (Rousseau) nor is it anything that could be conceived as a single will or represented symbolically by one (as, for example, by the will of a king, party, or ideological movement). Rather, a political process is the clash, composition, and creativity of many wills that seek a compromise that is different from what any one or even all of them specifically propose. The outcome of a political process is to create a compromise from a plurality of specific proposals. Anything that depreciates the plurality of willings in this process (especially anything that depreciates it in the name of an official ideology or a general will) destroys its political character. Politics, therefore, aims both to unify divergent willings while at the same time maintaining their divergent plurality. Its goal is not to dissolve disagreements, but to construct in relation to them a new complex alternative.

V. *The Process of Politicization*

Political activity is the most important of human creations. It is not natural, but cultural. The emergence of political society requires, therefore, the politicization of man.

The politicization of man can only take place where man learns to conceive of society in terms different from himself, that is, as something different from a "macrohuman being." As long as man thinks of society as the individual human writ large, he thinks non-politically. For example, in prepolitical times, society was conceived as a single "body" which had the king as its "head." In such a society, there would be no conception that there should be a "plurality of willings." Rather, the society—conceived as but a large human being—was thought to be properly governed by a single "head" just as the individual is.

In order for political society to exist, man must conceive of the social unit as unlike himself, i.e., as composed of a plurality of wills. But this must not be sheer plurality, for then there would be no society at all. Rather, man must conceive of society as the unity of a plurality of willings. The unification (more exactly, "communification") of the plurality of willings takes place through the political process.

It is possible, of course, for a society to be conceived as a *mere* plurality of willings. This is what occurs in sheer individual*ism*. In sheer individualism, each person conceives himself to be properly governed by only one will (his own!). In this sense, sheer individualism—as a principle of government—is identical with totalitarianism (for under totalitarianism each person also regards himself to be properly governed by only one will, i.e., another's).

Both totalitarianism and anarchism (the consequence of sheer individualism) are nonpolitical forms of government. Neither has attained to the essential idea of politics, namely, the idea of a complex social process that effects the communification of many wills. In political society, there is not simply the recognition of a plurality of willings (as in individualism), but also the recognition of the possibility of the communification of this plurality through the political process. Such a communification is not a mere balancing of the centrifugal pluralizing tendencies against the centripetal centralizing tendencies within a society. Rather, it is a new kind of willing embodied within a new social structure: the political community.

Within a society, there exist both centrifugal forces towards sheer plurality (ending in anarchism) and centripetal forces toward sheer centralism (ending in totalitarianism). These two forces actually reinforce one another for they are but two manifestations of the same governmental idea (namely, that man should be governed by but one will). The true alternative to both totalitarianism and anarchism is political society, for a political society originates out of a different conception of sovereignty, namely, the concept of a pluralized willing that is the communification of a plurality of wills.

VI. *Three Basic Political Institutions*

A political society, as a voluntary order that expresses the unity of a plurality of wills, exists only insofar as three basic institutions also exist. These institutions establish the procedures by which a political community is ordered and sustained. They are three: (1) intrinsic authority, (2) lawful justice, and (3) politics.

First, political society presupposes the existence of intrinsic authority, for its members obey its laws because they are "right" and not because they are enforced by "might." Intrinsic authority is authority that commends itself through men's acknowledging that it is (or has) right. Hence, intrinsic authority does not rely on sheer force or might to elicit obedience. To rely on sheer force would reduce the plurality of a society and, hence, its political character. For this reason, another principle of order must be established.

The special character of political society is seen in the institution of intrinsic authority, an institution that can only exist in a political context. In a nonpolitical society, citizens cannot freely act in conformity with the leader's command, for that command cannot be construed by them as properly their own command to themselves. Hence, in nonpolitical societies, the obedience of the people is rooted either in their lack of knowledge or will to do any other or it is compelled through the leader's monopoly on force and the implied threat that this force might be used in order to compel obedience to the government.

If, however, the ultimate foundation of law is such threat, the authority that gives law and that commands obedience is not intrinsic, that is, it is not an authority people obey freely because they have set it over themselves. When people set law over themselves, however, there exists intrinsic authority, and persons obey not because they are threatened, but because they acknowledge that it is right to obey. That is, they obey freely. It is this that preserves the plurality of willings in a society even while it orders them.

In a political society, authority can take this distinctive form (hence the state does not need to possess a monopoly of force). In a political society, the law is created by the citizens and actually expresses their own rule over themselves. When this occurs, men acknowledge the command of law as their own command to themselves and their obedience is free rather than compelled. That is, men obey authority because they acknowledge it as right. Such free obedience to intrinsic authority is one of the unique values of political society.

The second essential institution of political society is the administration of justice through law. Justice is the method of equitably ordering community in such a way that the essential dignity of all members is acknowledged and effectually sustained. Such political justice can only be institutionalized through law, for only through law can general conditions for human actions within community be established and those actions be equitably ordered. Moreover, only through law does the communitarian single will of the many receive sufficiently abstract expression to escape appearing as the monolithic (or arbitrary) will of a single person or party. It is the very generality and abstractness of law that renders it a fit symbol of political government (hence, a "government of law and not of men"). Moreover, the very character of the communitarian will requires that political justice be administered through law alone.

Political justice emerges in conjunction with the very pluralization through which a society is differentiated or becomes "political." In an undifferentiated society, all members participate in the same activity either directly or indirectly. For example, in primitive gathering societies, all members performed the same activity and lived the same way. Or, in a ritual group, all the members identify with one person (the "priests") and through this identification all empathetically perform the same activity and receive the same reward. In these undifferentiated societies, there is a natural equality: persons perform the same activity and receive the same return for that activity. When societies are differentiated, then labors and statuses are no longer naturally equal, but differ from one another. In this situation, an artificial, or political, equality must be created in order to replace the natural equality that has been lost. This artificial, or political, equality is created by a calculus of justice that seeks to weigh dissimilars in terms of an ideal of social "equity" and to distribute work and rewards through a third, or abstract, medium (e.g., money). Justice, operating through law, maintains both social equity and social differentiation. It is, therefore, a presupposition of political society.

The third essential institution of political society is politics. Politics is not simply the exercise of social power—for there is an exercise of social power that is non- or antipolitical. Politics seeks, rather, to exercise social power politically. It seeks to exercise power by differentiating and distributing it among many individuals and groups within a society, and then setting in motion a process of debate and conflict that aims for or ends in compromise. The first and fundamental act of politics is this differentiation and distribution of power that creates a pluralistic society. This is the primary step in politicization and it is only after this has taken place that the process of disagreement and conflict that aims at compromise can become socially creative.

The commitment to exercise social control through politics rather than through that depoliticization of a society that aims at reducing the plurality of its willings and absorbing them into a single will or ideology rests on the belief that a political group is both more creative socially and does greater justice to the peculiar dignity of man (his freedom). There is no question but that it is more difficult to control a society by politics rather than by depoliticizing it and trusting in the competence of a single will or group. The very difficulty of politics itself generates a latent antipolitical tendency, namely, the desire to reduce the number of centers of power in order to reduce the scope of the problem to be resolved. And such a reduction is always to be found, even in the most political societies. A perfectly politicized world is an ideal; we settle always for a situation that is more or less close to this.

To maintain the political character of a society, various institutions are necessary: the distinction of branches of government, the maintenance of multiple spheres of social loyalty (the state, the church, the family, a culture, a professional group), the establishment of higher and lower administrative units, the development of differing parties and social programs, etc. But all these institutions themselves are the expression of a fundamental conviction regarding man: that the plurality of wills, both individual and group, should be respected and allowed to shape the social process. This conviction is given expression in the idea that it is good for human beings to exercise freedom and have equal participation in society. The conviction that it is good for persons to be free and equal in this way is expressed, in modern political theory, through the proposal that all men have certain basic rights. The three rights stressed in the emergence of modern societies are freedom, equality, and brotherhood.

VII. The "Politicizing Rights of Man"

The rights guaranteed to all men by modern political society are affirmed to be inalienable, i.e., not abridgeable by society. Because they are inalienable, some have proposed that these rights describe man in an original state of nature ("natural rights"). However, it would be more accurate to say that a political society regards these rights as inalienable because they are the presupposition of its own existence as political. Were such rights to be abridged by a political society, it would destroy its own political character by reducing the plurality of its constituent wills. Because such rights exist necessarily in conjunction with political society, they are more properly called "civil" or "political rights." In fact, since the first function of such rights is to distribute power within a society and to maintain a plurality of centers of initiative, it would be most accurate to call them "politicizing rights."

Let us discuss three of these basic rights—freedom, equality, and brotherhood—in order to see how they contribute to the maintenance of a politicized society. Notice that "brotherhood," a right not usually affirmed together with the other two in the American context, is actually implied by them. To claim freedom and equality as political rights for oneself is also to acknowledge the rightness that they be claimed by others. Hence, when they are claimed as political rights, freedom and equality imply brotherhood.

First, then, the freedom of the members of a political society must be affirmed in order that there may exist a plurality of centers of initiative within it. This freedom, in the last analysis, cannot be limited to persons' choosing among already existing options, but it must include the right of each person to withdraw from the community entirely or to withdraw from particular activities when to engage in them would violate his sense of self. Only if this freedom of conscience (or freedom before God) exists in an institutionalized way within it can a society claim to be genuinely political, that is, claim to arise out of the free volition of its members. Such a protection of freedom exists in the United States, for example, by providing for conscientious objection against participation in wars lawfully decided upon by the government. Such conscientious objection is quite different from political objection—for political objection does not justify abrogating one's responsibility for participating in the ordinary institutions of society, but only allows the protection of a person's right to struggle, through political means, to alter the political decision of the community.

For much the same reason, it follows that there is no right of revolution within political society. This is the case because a political society provides its citizens with (a) the opportunity to make their wills effective through politics and thereby to shape the will of the community (which is all a free man can justly claim as his right) and (b) provides opportunity for withdrawal from participation in those programs that individual citizens find conscientiously objectionable. Revolution can only be claimed as a right where these freedoms have been violated. That is, revolution is a right only against a totalitarian state (or, perhaps, against the state insofar as it is totalitarian). The original American claim of a right to revolution against a government that did not allow the will of the governed to shape the laws that governed them in no way implies that Americans today retain the right to revolt against their own political community—insofar as this community provides them with all requisite political opportunities to shape the will of the nation.

The second presuppositional virtue of political society is equality. Equality, in this case, refers not to a principle of distribution, but to the acknowledgment that the worth of every will within the political community is neither greater nor less than every other will. This means that the conscience and freedom of each individual must be acknowledged and respected by the community as a whole and that justice be administered without respect to persons. Thus equality appears, first of all, as political equality. This does not mean the equality of opportunity for private gain, but means the equality of persons to have access to political institutions and to shape the public will.

A political society must insure to all its members the practical possibility of shaping its laws and institutions and of deciding its long term goals. This requires that it educate its citizens to the requisite level of knowledge, motivate them to seek and wield political responsibility, and free them from the penury that forces a man to use all of his energies simply to provide basic sustenance for himself (so that he has no energy left to consider his community or attempt to shape its common will). This means that schools, political education, access to courts and legal advice, basic medical care, and guaranteed employment or income must be provided by every political community for its members. Only if this is done is the essential political equality of the citizenry being effectively acknowledged. Moreover, it is important to realize that the provision of such things is not a charity or a benefit provided to individuals by a welfare state, but is a positive act of justice which is required of a political community if it is to sustain itself in being. It is precisely because such provisions express the structural values of political community that their creation takes precedence over any teleological value or long range goal—however laudable such a goal might be. In America today, this means that adequate schools, political education, health care, access to the courts and legal advice, guaranteed income, and so forth must be provided before space exploration (as one example!) is further continued. Otherwise the credibility of America as a just society ceases to exist—and its citizens will be thereby justified to engage in violent revolution against it.

Finally, a political community presupposes brotherhood as a third constitutive virtue in its citizens. By brotherhood is meant that feeling or expression of loyalty of men to one another through which members of a community acknowledge both their independence from one another and also their essential community with one another. The affirmation of brotherhood is that men with whom I disagree are still men to whom I owe loyalty and who owe reciprocal loyalty. In spite of all social division, Americans owe loyalty to one another.

The sense of brotherhood, or loyalty to one another, is the foundation of the acknowledgment of reciprocal rights and responsibilities within political community. Brotherhood is that through which the essential unity of the community is affirmed (even while acknowledging, at the same time, the plurality of its membership). Brotherhood is the communitarian symbol of solidarity. A political community, lacking any single head, finds the symbol of its unity in the idea of brotherhood and in the experience of loyalty to one another that flows from this idea. It is an evidence of the growing political disintegration within American society that brotherhood today is regarded as a banal piety without concrete social meaning.

Without the sense of brotherhood, the mere acknowledgment of the freedom and equality of persons in society will be insufficient to create political community. These latter two virtues, or character strengths, must be supplemented by the affirmation of the brotherhood of the members (or loyalty or solidarity of the members with one another) if community is to come into existence. For this reason, every person in a political community has the *right* to demand that its other members acknowledge him as a brother and maintain loyalty to him—while he, for his part, must acknowledge them as brothers and maintain faith with them and his community. The value of brotherhood is the indispensable foundation of all political life, and the failure to give this value equal emphasis alongside freedom and equality has led to the development in America of an exaggerated tendency towards individualism.

VIII. *Public Communications and Polyconsciousness*

Political society comes into existence through the activity of a plurality of wills, through whose conflict and compromise a common will is created. The presupposition of such politics is not simply that there exists a plurality of wills, but that each of these wills has responsibility for considering the good of the community as a whole. This responsibility does not, of course, imply that any individual citizen has the duty to override the rights of others nor the responsibility to provide direct care for those in need. But it does imply that each citizen (or political unit) has the obligation to consider the common good and to seek, in the light of his judgment, to shape the institutions of the community as a whole. It implies that the political activity of every citizen will not be directed solely to the protection of his private interests (as if there were some magic mechanism that would create a just society out of the mere conflict of private interests). It means that the political activity of each citizen will include a concern for the good of the community as a whole—for which he has a responsibility.

A political community does not come into existence merely through the acknowledgment of the separate existence of a plurality of wills. If it *could* originate in this way (a nineteenth century mechanistic theory!), then it would be proper for each person to concern himself with his own private interests. Moreover, although there might be an ordered society when each will seeks to defend only its own private interests and comes into conflict with other wills insofar as they encroach upon its private sphere, there could be, in such circumstances, no political community. Political community presupposes not simply the existence of a plurality of wills, but also that each of these wills is vested with the responsibility to judge about and to seek the establishment of the common good. Politics, therefore, is not simply a clash of wills that are defending a plurality of private interests, but *is the clash of wills in their struggle to ascertain and establish the social good and create the order of community as a whole.* To think of politics merely as the clash of private interests evidences the depreciating effect of unrestrained individualism upon American society.

The very plurality of political society, however, has been seen by many as incompatible with the idea of a social, or common, good. Radical individualism has sometimes been conceived to mean that not only is there no common social good, but also that there could not be one because individuals are so different from one another that they cannot even understand one another's point of view. On the other hand, there are those who argue that a society can only exist on the basis of a commonality and likeness among its members. Only if the citizens share common commitments and similar values can, so the reasoning goes, a society be one.

The question that must be raised is whether there is a way of creating a community that does not depreciate or qualify the plurality of differences among its members. What if people are so different that they are not alike in the most basic respects? How can people even understand one another if they don't share the same values and point of view? If a society is to become political, it must deal practically with this problem.

In part, the answer is that in political societies it is necessary to develop a new kind of human consciousness. This new consciousness must be more highly differentiated and possess a greater capacity to bear plurality within itself. It must be "polyconsciousness." A person living in a political society must possess more power of empathy; he must be an Empathic Man. Such empathic persons are able to identify imaginatively with those who are different from themselves and, in this way, to bear a higher degree of inward contrariety. Political persons must be politicized even within their inward consciousnesses.

The primary institution for developing this new capacity for empathy within a society is the communications media. In a political society, the media's function is to create empathic images through which its citizens may learn to identify with the complexity and plurality of social life. Two media functions can be distinguished. First, there is the responsibility of the communications media to create empathic images and information that make it possible for members of one social group to identify with members of another social group. In this way, the public media help develop a social consciousness of the plurality and complexity of life. They maintain the awareness of a society as political, as containing variety and contraries; and they help people understand that the process that aims at defining the social good must aim at compromise in every particular case.

To the extent that the media have developed images of social plurality and the contraries within a society, the citizens will be sufficiently polyconscious and political. The media can operate, however, in a non- or antipolitical way; they can create not images of complexity, but images that have a monolithic consistency. When this occurs, the citizenry tends towards the one-dimensional consciousness that is unable to bear social complexity and prefers to resolve social problems in a nonpolitical way. For this reason, there must be not merely large public communications networks within a society, but also publishing, TV, and communications outlets that are specifically aimed at heightening the self-consciousness of distinctive social groups. There must be a "press" for each and every social group that cannot relate on a person-to-person basis alone— for without such a press, groups lose their sense of identity under the deluge of images promulgated by the larger public communications network.

Where subgroups within a society suffer from media deprivation, they lose their power to engage in political action. Media deprivation depoliticizes a society. For this reason, a political society requires both larger public networks and also vigorous local and group-specific presses.

IX. *The Political Meanings of Transcendence*

The religious faith of political community is faith in the transcendent. That is, the faith of political community is precisely that which excludes the absolutizing of any single will, group, or set of temporal goals. This means, too, that the faith of political community opposes all nonpolitical and immanentalistic forms of religion.

Not religion as such, but faith in the transcendent, is the foundation of political community and its undergirding values. Actually, there are many forms of religion that do not involve faith in a transcendent reality, but only trust in some person, immanent principle, or temporal program. (Every ideology is such an immanent principle.) To deify any immanent principle leads eventually to totalitarianism and the breakdown of political society. It does so because the immanent principle is made into the center of society so that the society itself no longer stands under judgment.

Political society expresses its faith in the transcendent by its refusal to establish an official religion. To "establish" a religion is to make a particular symbolization of the experience of the ultimate into a program for society. For a political community to refuse to establish an official religion is not a form of hostility to religion, rather it is a way of society's expressing a faith in God. For by refusing to establish a religion, society brings even religion under the judgment of a transcendent higher principle: Truth, Justice, God.

These considerations lead us to see why the essential faith of political community need not be presented in any particular religious form. This is so because not religion per se, but faith in the transcendent is the principle of political society—and faith in the transcendent can take many (even nonreligious!) forms.

The symbolizations of the transcendent are various and, because they often take the form of criticisms of immanentalistic and idolatrous religion, have traditionally appeared in novel, even atheistic, forms. For example, the ancient Hebrews and the early Christians were called atheists because they refused to bow down before graven images or worship political authorities as divine. Though Judaism and Christianity at first appeared as atheisms, they finally became the animating forces that produced political pluralistic community. Therefore, when today we see the emergence of new symbolic representations of the transcendent—representations that are frequently presented as criticisms of traditional religion—we may as well anticipate that these symbolizations are new vital affirmations of political society's faith in God as to suppose that they are mere secular idolatries. There will be no difficulty distinguishing among these symbolisms if we remember that the crucial mark of political community is its affirmation of a transcendent reality that judges all temporal things rather than the mere affirmation of religion per se.

In fact, the symbolizations of the transcendent have varied within the Judaeo-Christian tradition and have found three different forms of political institutionalization. All of these institutionalizations of the experience of transcendence have become part of American society and account, in large part, for its extraordinary pluralistic character and complexity.

The first conception of transcendence was the ancient Hebrew idea that no ruler or ruling group is an adequate "image" of God. In Israel, the consequence of this denial that any man can claim to represent the will of God is that all rulers came under the criticism of others—who spoke out against injustice in their role as "prophets."

In ancient Israel, the idea of God as the sole true sovereign ruler relativized every earthly ruler. It was a way of affirming the finitude of all men. The belief in man's finitude led, in Israel, to the institutionalization of prophetic criticism of all rulers, that is, to the institutionalization of a "countersovereignty" that scrutinized and checked the sovereignty of the kings. This same idea finds its embodiment in American political life through the institutionalization of a system of checks and balances whereby the powers of government are checked, in part, by other powers within government itself.

The second symbolization of the transcendent arose in early Christianity and became the basis of the Orthodox and Catholic experience of God. In early Christianity, there was, for the first time, the emergence of the belief that man himself has a supernatural social destiny, the belief that man is made to have communion with Christ in a "kingdom that is not of this world." The experience of a transcendent, supernatural social order meant, for early Christians, that they could no longer conceive of the ultimate goal of their lives in temporal terms. It means that they denied that any earthly society, however utopian and perfect, could ever meet all the needs of man. The political consequence of this conviction was the claim, by Orthodox and Catholic Christianity, that society must give up total sovereignty over time, space, and property and must allow some time, space, and property to be ruled freely by institutions which already manifested and were devoted to the pursuit of supernatural community.

By stressing the fact that man has a transtemporal social destiny that already is being lived and prepared for in this world, the Orthodox and Catholic Churches relativized the claim of every society to be able to fulfill the full range of human needs. It relegated every earthly set of goals to a penultimate status and thereby furthered pluralized the structure of political community. The political consequence of this faith in man's supernatural end was the Church's claim to exist as an autonomous institution that possesses full sovereignty over its own activities. Practically, this means that the state must allow to religious institutions exemption from the taxation of property and that it must also lay aside sufficient time and space within the community at large so that ecclesiastical institutions may engage in worship and other activities expressive of man's supernatural end.

The third Judaeo-Christian symbolization of transcendence has been especially developed within the Protestant tradition. This symbolization stresses the uniqueness of every person, the absolute privacy of individual conscience and purely personal communication, and the right of every man to define his own fulfillment and seek his own happiness. To affirm the uniqueness of persons means not simply that God transcends and is uniquely different from every other person, but that all created persons transcend and are uniquely different from one another. The uniqueness of persons sets a limitation on scientific, or generic, knowledge—for uniqueness cannot be known or dealt with under any rule or in any discursive way. The uniqueness of persons can be, at best, acknowledged and encountered. In the words of Martin Buber, the unique person is a "thou" and not an "it." This means that there must exist a realm of personal relation and human privacy that stands quite free from scientific— or even social—manipulation.

Just as the consequence of the Israelite view of transcendence was the political institutionalization of "countersovereignties" and the separation of powers and just as the consequence of the Orthodox-Catholic view of the supernatural end of man was the exemption of churches from governmental oversight in order to allow certain times, spaces, and properties to be devoted to transtemporal ends, so the consequence of the Protestant experience of the uniqueness of persons also has found a political institutionalization. In American society, the faith in the uniqueness of persons leads to the acknowledgment that every human being has the right to privacy, to the sole government of his own conscience, and to claim for his own as much time, space, and property as is necessary to maintain the existence of the private psychic sphere.

The existence of this private sphere, as the corollary of the affirmation that every man is unique, sets the same limitation on overall political planning as does the existence of an ecclesiastical-supernatural sphere. Just as the political community as a whole cannot claim to determine all the time, space, property, and order of its institutions—for it must leave churches free to exist and pursue their own activities—so the political community cannot claim to determine all its individual citizens' goals, since they must also be allowed to define and seek their own goals within the private sphere. The political community at large must allow this right to be exercised by leaving sufficient time and space unplanned so that individual persons may have the opportunity to do significant planning for themselves. The allocation of significant amounts of time and space to individual persons sets a necessary limitation on all political aspirations towards total planning. Moreover, since the existence of such free time and space has, heretofore, been severely limited by economic exigencies, it now becomes a matter of first priority that the development of economic abundance be coordinated with the allocation of more and more time and space to the planning and disposal of individuals. If, instead, economic abundance goes hand in hand with increased planning in the public sphere—so that persons not gain increased power to dispose of their own time, space, and psychic freedom—the foundations of political society will be jeopardized.

X. *Civil Religion or Politics?*

In this essay we have stressed that a political society maintains its structure through institutions that multiply its centers of initiative and pluralize its decision-making process: intrinsic authority, lawful justice, and politics; the politicizing rights of freedom, equality, and brotherhood; the media's production of empathic images; the rejection of ideology and established religions—these are the elements of political society.

Some have argued that commitment to these elements of political society is itself something ultimate, a kind of "civil religion" that stands alongside the particular religions of the society. They argue thus because they claim that belief in the elements of political society implies some generalized affirmation about the destiny of man and his fulfillment on earth. Political society, so their reasoning goes, involves a faith in certain ultimate values and this faith must be given mythic-ritual expression in the history and life of a people.

In order to clarify the issue at stake, let us here recall the original distinction between two types of values: teleological and structural-procedural. The former determine our goals and are directional; the latter determine the way we decide and pursue our goals—and even how we decide our teleological values. It is not the case that a political society requires that its members agree with respect to teleological values or conceptions of human happiness and fulfillment. A political society requires only that its members (who can and do disagree on teleological values and ultimate goals) be willing to interact politically enough to compromise their differences so that a social order can exist. A political society, therefore, requires agreement only on structural-procedural and not on teleological values.

Symbolizations of the origins and destiny of a people are not the common term that holds a political society together. For example, it is not necessary that all Americans appropriate the Revolution as their history or identify with Abraham Lincoln as an archetypal hero. Such historical and eschatological symbolizations may unite a society, but they also tend to undercut its plurality and qualify its political character. Such teleological symbolisms are found in nonpolitical societies and function as civil religions; i.e., they present images of man's origin and *telos* in mythic-ritual form. Teleological symbol systems always presuppose that society is not a plurality of different agents, but a single organic whole.

In a political society, there must be something that articulates and symbolizes the unity of the society. But it cannot be a civil religion. First, this is because the thing that articulates the unity of a political society must focus on common procedural values and institutions alone, and must exclude (even oppose) all teleological values and images of a society's origin and end. Second, the thing that articulates the unity of a political society must affirm the absolute plurality of existence and, in this way, oppose all images that portray society as a single "whole." Third, the thing that articulates the unity of political society must reject the mythic-religious mode of discourse and must protect itself against the intellectual tendency to utilize God-symbols or wholistic images of ultimacy. (The ordinary way a political society does this is to bestow upon its particular religious and idealistic groups a monopoly on "God symbolism.")

What is this thing by which we articulate the unity of a political society? It is politics itself (elections, debates, judicial acts) and *political philosophy*. Precisely because the political process cannot be hypostatized as a single general will, but must be conceived as a contingent system of relations that is created as various agents choose to interact and compromise with one another, the symbolic level on which it must be described is not that of religious myth, but that of practical philosophy. We seek to describe it in terms of the contingent laws and pragmatic regularities in terms of which persons and groups interact and negotiate. These are abstract names: authority, law, justice, freedom. Such ideas do not represent any cosmic whole; they merely describe the general principles in terms of which people act politically. We do not inculcate, or symbolize, such ideas by myth, nor dare we canonize any particular case of them. Rather, we operate with them daily and through this daily operation learn what they mean. They become, in this way, not the ultimate mythic-vision, but the habits and ordinary morality of a people.

Politics can exist only when it is understood that politics is not religion. Politics has nothing to do with visions of man's ideal end (eschatology), and attempts to change the form of the political process by demanding that it produce utopia rather than compromise means its very destruction. Politics does not solve the ultimate questions of life, will not bring salvation, cannot make men happy. Its goal is more modest, but no less essential. Politics allows persons and groups that have different aspirations to live together in relative peace and to cooperate in limited ways for the sake of specific finite benefits. Whenever politics seeks to be more than this, it must inevitably become far less.

WILLI OELMÜLLER

4. The Limitations
of Social Theories

Translated by Joan Lockwood and Herbert W. Richardson
Introduction by Joan Lockwood

Introduction

In "The Limitations of Social Theories," Willi Oelmüller examines three contemporary social theories and seeks to show how each leaves certain problems unresolved. These unresolved problems, he argues, relate to the essential limits of social theories, to what they can and what they cannot legitimately aspire to accomplish. In principle, social theories presuppose determinate conceptions of the human person, the goal of human life, and the phenomenon of evil or negativity. It is these more general notions which limit the application of social theories. For this reason, Oelmüller wants to focus directly on these notions and to develop an independent "practical philosophy" that "seeks to grasp the conditions of human action and the means by which individuals and groups realize their goals."

In his essay, Oelmüller analyzes the problems left outstanding in three contemporary social theories: the "critical rationalism" developed by the English philosopher, Karl Popper; the "critical theory" developed by the neo- and post-Marxist group of thinkers called the Frankfurt School; and the communications-and-systems theories developed principally by such North American thinkers as Talcott Parsons and Noam Chomsky. An understanding of "critical rationalism" and "critical theory" is particularly necessary for an appreciation of this essay.

"Critical rationalism" is the name for the distinctive method of postpositivist social analysis developed since the 1930s by Karl Popper, Hans Albert, and others. Karl Popper, like the philosopher Wittgenstein, emigrated from Vienna to Great Britain before the Second World War. The intellectual background of both men included study of the positivism of the Vienna School, a philosophy which aimed to restrict human knowledge to description of empirical events or sense data. In this positivist tradition, claims about value or the nature of man and the goals of human life were held to be nonrational, i.e., not susceptible of being argued or proved by methods yielding real "knowledge." Values and metaphysics were, accordingly, relegated to the realm of belief or taste.

In the 1920s and 1930s many thinkers felt it necessary to try to counter the Nazis' myths and truth claims by regenerating the tradition of rational criticism. Positivism, it was felt, gave an indirect support to the Nazis' insistence on the irrationality of human life—on "blood" and "myth" rather than reason as the final court of appeal. Karl Popper's work must be seen in this political context. Popper attempted to develop a "postpositivist" philosophy which would lay the foundation for a rational criticism of skepticism, irrationalism, and ideology. Popper argued that not merely our sense experience, but also our value commitments are open to rational criticism, though not ultimately to rational justification. In other words, Popper refused to set reason up as a new "scientific authority" which would take precedence over "traditional authorities." Reason, for Popper, is not essentially a principle of authority or final justification; rather, it is a principle of criticism against all claims to finality and all authority—even rational authority. Hence, Popper's critical rationalism is, first of all, criticism of rationalism.

In his *Logic of Scientific Discovery* (1935) and later in *The Open Society and Its Enemies* (1945), Popper shows that the critical notion of reason implies a social context which is open to conflict and capable of bearing continuing change. It is this social situation that both establishes and protects the critical activity of reason. By linking thought and democratic society in this way, Popper perpetuates and further advances the tradition of John Dewey. Hence, it is not surprising that his work should have attracted such widespread attention in the American world. For example, Mario Bunge has edited an important collection of essays on critical rationalism: *The Critical Approach to Science and Philosophy* (Glencoe, 1964).

The second school of social thought which Oelmüller discusses is "critical theory." Critical theory refers to the distinctive method of neo- and post-Marxist social analysis developed after the First World War by a distinguished group of thinkers who first gathered in Frankfurt-am-Main, Germany. Included in this group were Max Horkheimer, Theodore Adorno, Erich Fromm, Herbert Marcuse, Leo Lowenthal, and others. (Fromm was later to leave it.) Closely allied in spirit to these Frankfurt thinkers were George Lukacs and Ernst Bloch.

These men, though Marxist in orientation, attempted to develop a more comprehensive method. First, they rejected the nineteenth-century Marxist view of history (labelling it "objectivist" and "petrified ideology"). Alternatively, they stressed the impossibility of any general theory of history, rather affirming that all knowledge is created by man in the "force field" of a unique situation. Second, they stressed the creative character of all knowledge and cultural activity, opposing the notion that knowledge and culture are *passive reflections* of economic relationships (as nineteenth-century Marxism had proposed) or social environment (as certain American educators suggest). Consequently, these Frankfurt theorists studied not only economic, but all human, relationships: sexuality (Fromm), politics (von Neumann), mass media (Lowenthal), music (Adorno), literature (Benjamin), philosophy (Marcuse), and sociology (Horkheimer). Third, they reappropriated the "early Marx" and argued that the dialectical, or "conflict," element is rooted in man as such; that is, the impulse to revolutionary critique does not originate in the economic process, but is the ineradicable mark of human existence. For this reason, the Frankfurt school engaged in a constant systematic criticism of all attempts to harmonize or "prematurely order" human life. Herbert Marcuse's *Eros and Civilization* is, in this respect, atypical. More faithful to the Frankfurt movement is Max Horkheimer's assertion that critical theory resembles the Old Testament affirmation that nothing in this world is perfect or beyond judgment—not excepting utopian visions.

The significance of the Frankfurt School lies in its insistence that knowledge is *never* descriptive, but is an interaction between persons governed by "interests" and social situations. Moreover, the process of cultural production (including the production of knowledge) is always dialectical; it always contains an element of self-negation. Armed with this conception of dialectical-and-interested reason, the Frankfurt School has undertaken a radical criticism of modern science and philosophical positivism, including the ideal of objectivity and openness presupposed in Karl Popper's critical rationalism.

In his essay, Oelmüller develops an internal critique of critical theory and critical rationalism. He attempts to show that there is a discrepancy between the goals these social theories profess and the methods they propose, and that this discrepancy prevents them from accomplishing what they intend. Oelmüller's criticism of systems theory, is however, somewhat different in that here he argues that the very conception of society as a system is fundamentally reductionistic. Opposing this view, he defends the notion that society is composed of a plurality of autonomous subjects and afflicted by an internal negativity, or evil; thus, he argues, a systems analysis of behavior is unable to give an adequate account of human decision and action.

The Limitations of Social Theories

I. *Practical Philosophy in the Light of Theories of Science and Society*

It appears that the historical development of scientific understanding and human emancipation has today come to a standstill. Many have come to regard this development as mere middle-class ideology. Our awareness of new problems in technological society, together with such scientific developments as hermeneutics and empirical analysis, seem to confirm this judgment. However, the very tendencies which today seem to oppose the development of scientific understanding and human emancipation can be interpreted to be part of this process itself. Since the time of the Enlightenment, opposing and antithetical tendencies have been judged to be, dialectically, a part of the very drive towards increased freedom. A process is seen to include not only what furthers it, but also what apparently impedes it. Hence, classical German philosophy saw the analysis of these impediments and imperfections to be the first step in any further advance. However, advance today is becoming increasingly difficult—as formerly "self-evident" assumptions have lost their self-evident character.

If philosophy desires to make clear once more the Enlightenment understanding, it faces a methodological problem that is pregnant with consequences. It can no longer proceed on the Aristotelian assumption of a common sense immediately visible in the self-understanding and actions of individuals and groups. Nor can philosophy dare to presume that within the dominant social sciences there exists a general consensus as to the goals of science and the criteria of human freedom. In these circumstances what is philosophy to do?

One possibility is for philosophy to recover the presuppositions and problematic of a particular philosophical tradition; it might, for example, reinstate the outlook of classical German philosophy. Alternatively, it might engage in a critical dialogue with contemporary social and scientific theories in order to elucidate the traditional presuppositions and problems of the modern enlightenment movement, which would in turn be reevaluated and transformed. It is the latter approach that will be taken in this essay.

Revitalization of the process of scientific emancipation requires that we undertake to do practical philosophy once more. According to Aristotle, practical philosophy is that inquiry which, like ethics, economics, and politics, seeks to grasp the conditions of human action and the means by which individuals and groups realize their goals. Until the eighteenth century, practical philosophy remained an independent discipline, despite the many social changes occurring prior to that time. Only with the upsurge of modern science and technology, commerce, and bureaucracy—i.e., with the emergence of the modern state—did the tradition of an autonomous practical philosophy come to an end. Indeed, wherever philosophy itself was touched by these social changes, the very idea of practical philosophy disappeared. Today, however, practical philosophy is being resuscitated by Marxists who want to get beyond dogma-encrusted Marxism as well as by political thinkers intent on rehabilitating this now forgotten way of thinking.

The starting point for the following discussion is the fact that current theories of science and society concerned with individuals, groups, and political action are actually doing what practical philosophy can and ought to be doing at the present time. Consequently, if practical philosophy is to help advance scientific understanding and human freedom, it must formulate its ideas in conversation with certain contemporary theories: the "critical rationalism" of Popper and Albert; the "critical theory" of Horkheimer, Adorno, and Habermas; linguistic theory and "the logic of communication"; and sociopolitical "systems analysis." In our discussion of the various ways in which the above theories contribute to the search for the presuppositions and conditions of the modern enlightenment movement we shall observe that they leave unanalyzed a certain part of the problem, i.e., they leave a certain residue that suggests a direction for further investigation. Naturally, it is impossible to discuss each of these theories exhaustively or to explore the relations among them.

II. *The Unresolved Problems within the "Critical Rationalism" of Popper and Albert*

Unlike the logical positivism of the early Wittgenstein and Carnap, the critical rationalism of Popper and Albert does not in principle exclude the ethical point of view or consider ethical propositions as meaningless. Wittgenstein and Carnap oriented their work in terms of the language and method of a specific mathematical logic, formulating from within this perspective norms for all thinking. By these means they hoped to eliminate those senseless questions which crop up whenever thought is seduced by metaphysics or by sheer linguistic confusion. For Wittgenstein there can be "no ethical propositions, since propositions can express nothing higher."[1] Similarly, for the early Carnap, the "supposed propositions of metaphysics, value theory and ethics are . . . pseudopropositions."[2]

Although Popper and Albert agree that "ethics is no science," they propose that "while there is no rational scientific basis for ethics, there is an ethical basis for science and rationality."[3] In explicating the meaning of this proposition, Popper and Albert hark back to the eighteenth-century Enlightenment traditions in order to develop ethical criteria for science and society outside the influence of logical positivism. Consequently, it is hardly meaningful to allow the vague and frequently pejorative notions of "positivism" and "neopositivism" to set the context for discussion of Popper and Albert's work. The positivism controversy has established that much.

Popper and Albert defend their return to the early Enlightenment by invoking the destruction of "the tradition of rational philosophy and, with this, the tradition of rationality in its broadest sense" in our own "postrational and postcritical age."[4] In undertaking to criticize those scientific and social tendencies retarding progress and to formulate social ideals, both Popper and Albert find it necessary to align themselves with the traditions of the Enlightenment. "Modern society," writes Albert, "need not reject tradition. But, one of the most important traditions for modern society ought to be the tradition of critical rationality, which is one of the most ancient traditions of the West."[5]

To Popper and Albert, this critical Enlightenment tradition is undermined by a philosophy of language that short-circuits legitimate philosophical investigations as "pure linguistic misconceptions."[6] This critical tradition is also vitiated by linguistic philosophy which, through "methods for the construction of artificial models of speech" and "analysis of ordinary language," produces "great systems of language games" which are worthless to scientific and social processes.[7] The other enemies of the critical tradition are "philosophy of history" and "ideology" (a reference to Hegel and Marx) along with relativism in its historical, psychological, and sociological forms. In contemporary Germany, the critical tradition is eroded above all else by the "antimodern" hermeneutical and dialectical thinking that has "penetrated the theological world."[8] (These ideas are further elaborated by Albert in his debates with representatives of "critical theory.")

Popper and Albert state explicitly that their decision against irrationalism and for rationality, and, hence, for the ongoing development of the critical tradition, rests on a fundamental moral decision. It rests on a faith in reason, a faith for which one can give illuminating, but not compelling, arguments. In their view, someone who opts for such a procedure of rational testing and modification of scientific hypotheses, practical norms, and social and political institutions cannot ground that option on a prior knowledge legitimated by metaphysics and philosophy of history. Science of itself cannot, according to Popper and Albert, furnish an adequate foundation for "the ideal of the pure search for truth" which is regulative for pure rationality. If science wants to be more than a correct use of formal-methodological rules for technical manipulation, then it must rest on extrascientific presuppositions which are mediated by history. "Our motivation and our pure scientific ideals—as well as the ideal of the pure search for truth —are anchored deeply within extrascientific and, in part, religious values. The objective value-free scientist is not the ideal scientist.[9]

For critical rationalism, the ideal intended by the "ethical basis of science and rationality," i.e., the knowledge of truth and the realization of a humane community, remains a regulative idea. It is a utopian anticipation which can be made intelligible only through critical recollection and transformation of Enlightenment traditions. Moreover, decisions concerning attainable goals for personal, social, and political action and the choice of means for their realization cannot be based on scientific knowledge. These decisions are dependent not only on extrascientific interests and needs, but also on the creative imagination of those involved. So, Albert affirms that "neither science nor a normative system of premises can replace the creative imagination that is indispensable for the solution of new problems. For this reason, every attempt to anticipate a human action in a deductive way (*more geometrico*) is open to failure."[10]

Popper and Albert do not confine their model of rationality to a specific discipline. It applies equally to the sciences and the humanities, and in addition, provides the decision-making norms for politics and society. Popper's development of this model is found in his book *Logic of Scientific Discovery*. Here he attempts to develop a method for generating scientific progress. He begins by denying (1) the capacity of human reason to arrive at absolute knowledge (e.g., Plato and Hegel) and (2) the existence of an absolute starting point for knowledge (e.g., empiricism or the dogmatic rationalism of the eighteenth century). "The older scientific ideal of absolutely certain knowledge (*episteme*) has proved to be an idol. The demand for objectivity leads to every scientific statement's being provisional. A scientific proposition can be tested, but every test is relative since it is a function of other equally provisional statements."[11] If critical rationalism attacks untenable hypotheses or unresolved scientific problems in order to develop better, though provisional, solutions, it must begin with certain basic principles that are conventionally acknowledged to be true and that have maintained themselves to the present, even though in principle they can be falsified. Hence, Popper asserts that "every test of a theory, irrespective of whether it verifies or falsifies it, must accept certain basic axioms. If these axioms are not explicitly acknowledged, then the process of verification is pointless. However, we are never logically compelled to maintain any special set of premises or to surrender any particular test. Rather, every premise can be reverified by deduction from other premises, in which circumstances the same theory must be employed again or else supplemented. This method never arrives at a natural end. If we desire an outcome, we must declare ourselves to be provisionally satisfied at one or another point."[12]

The employment of this rationalistic model of society and politics presupposes that scientific and social conflicts can be resolved by means of discussion and democratic voting procedures. In Popper's view, the final goal of society and politics is the attainment of an "open society" (in the sense of liberal democracy), achieved through dialogue, struggle against prejudice and all forms of totalitarian dictatorship, and establishment of liberal institutions. Albert, in his latest writings, sees more clearly than Popper the difficulties entailed in applying the rationalistic model to scientific and technological societies. He regards this model as presenting a "specific danger" for many countries with weak liberal and democratic traditions. The danger lies in the transition of these countries to the life-style of "postindustrial society," a life-style shaped largely by the sciences. "The alliance," says Albert, "of dogmatic-ideological control with the technological utilization of knowledge, whether under Marxist or other auspices, is a phenomenon that should not be taken lightly."[13]

The critical rationalism of Popper and Albert wishes to put the damper on irrationalism and "decisionism" in the sciences and in social and political action. This does not mean that critical rationalism holds to the illusory belief that these can ever be fully eliminated. Popper and Albert insist that the process of reasoning should not be brought to conclusion too soon, whether by extra-scientific taboos or by rational prescriptions for thought. Nevertheless, if this appeal of Popper and Albert to the Enlightenment is to be taken seriously, there remain certain unresolved problems within their theory of science and society which lead to criticism and further discussion. This residue of unresolved problems will take on special clarity in the following three points.

1. Contrary to its own claims, Popper's *Logic of Scientific Discovery* can neither provide an adequate explanation of the pro-

cedures of individual sciences nor offer specific criteria for their criticism and reform. Popper's attempt to gain objectivity for the *Logic* by introducing quasi-ontological "facts" or "social realities in the social world that correspond to physical realities in the physical world"[14] ends up in an objectivism. Such objectivism regresses to a pre-Kantian understanding of the conditions of science insofar as it does not include an account of the relation of reason to its own thinking which obtains in every critical activity as well as in science. That procedure of truth finding through experimental verification which, according to critical rationalism, is uniquely adapted to every science may be appropriate in the natural sciences where the "object" can be manipulated and operated on, but does not extend to all methods in the empirical analytical sciences, e.g., to those of ordinary language philosophy; and it cannot be the procedure of those sciences whose constitutive object is known through history, e.g., theology and the hermeneutical disciplines. Moreover, Popper's distinguishing of a "purely scientific interest in the truth" from extrascientific interests and valuations is unclear and loaded with contradiction. While, on the one hand, Popper, to avoid naturalism and indifference, requires the affirmation of definite values mediated through the traditions of the Enlightenment, on the other hand, he demands that extrascientific presuppositions be eliminated from the scientific process. He argues that "such trivial factors as, for example, the social or ideological point of view of the researcher eliminate themselves in time, although they naturally always play a short term role.[15] This inconsistency tends to blind us to the economic, military, social, and political interests which actually determine the character of contemporary science. Today, decision-making procedures in the sciences and in all research dependent on the economy and the state operate not according to any logic which arises out of a "pure scientific interest in the truth." Rather, they are widely dependent on extrascientific, military, and national interests. Critical rationalism has not, to the present time, developed adequate criteria for identifying and diagnosing this set of relations. The increasingly urgent question that Popper's *Logic* does not answer is whether the science and research which seeks to plan everything that can be planned and done is really serving social progress, i.e., is really serving the removal of hunger, the overcoming of oppression, and the prevention of war. Nor does Popper's logic help us tackle the problem of what should be planned and done. The criteria offered by critical rationalism's model of rationality are not sufficient for understanding the methods within individual sciences or for analyzing and criticizing society, politics, or the scientific enterprise.

2. Application of Popper's model of rationality to science and society presumes an insight into the relation of theory to practice, of science to the technologically controlled world, that is lacking even among many exponents of analytical methods. Albert himself criticizes those defenders of analysis who so accentuate the autonomy of scientific knowledge that they scarcely admit a relationship between philosophy and politics. "They so reduce philosophy to a theory of knowledge oriented to the purely scientific that they fail to discern that broad meaning of the models of rationality which is operative in scientific research. Consequently, they interpret the principle of value-free science so narrowly that it becomes a way of exempting political opinions and decisions from criticism."[16]

Application of Popper's model further assumes that a consensus about how to settle disagreements concerning goals and priorities can be arrived at by the cooperation of all interested parties in the problem-solving process. For this to be the case, the hoped-for outcome of the social-historical process (according to Popper's theory) would already have to exist—namely, an open society of mature and enlightened citizens who are prepared to resolve conflicts and meet needs in a reasonable manner without resorting to force or oppression. However, in social and political decision making, we need concrete objectives, goals that have more than a functional-pragmatic meaning. The purely functional conception of truth which Popper is proposing in his "open society" is too formal and open-ended to guide social and political decisions.

3. Popper and Albert's criticism of trends in contemporary science and society from a stance within the traditions of the Enlightenment assumes that neither the decision to be rational nor the call for an open society can be provided with full rational justification. Now, even our agreement with critical rationalism

on many points does not allay the necessity of our asking some questions about the goal of an "open society." What is at issue here is not the existence or nonexistence of an "open society" in the West or the Third World, but its desirability in principle. What we should fear, as Albert rightly sees, is that in a technologically controlled world whose liberal traditions are disappearing or have disappeared the open society becomes a one-dimensional, manipulated "Brave New World" in which resignation, boredom, and brutality reign, freedom having been trammeled. Critical rationalism's plea remains abstract and ineffective in the absence of adequate guidelines for the modern enlightenment movement, guidelines which help us preserve our freedom when it is being threatened. It is vacuous to place hope in "an approach to the truth" if, when faced with the unresolved conflicts among socialist and capitalist societies and the Third World, we merely confine ourselves to a pragmatic and functional definition of truth. The rationality that Popper and Albert circumscribe with the terms "exactitude," "precision," "mathematization," "efficiency," "simplicity," and "relevance" accords with the methods of the natural sciences and technology, but is too one-dimensional for a discussion of political and social goals. And so, the call for a critical rationalism becomes merely an appeal to the maturity of the immature who don't even know how to discern or criticize those powers which keep them from being mature. These remaining problems within critical rationalism will drive it eventually to further reflection.

III. *The Unresolved Problems within the "Critical Theory" of Horkheimer, Adorno, and Habermas*

Critical theory was developed in the 1930s by Max Horkheimer and Theodore Adorno, both professors later associated with the University of Frankfurt. Their ideas were formed in the context of their encounter with fascism, Stalinism, and the positivism and pragmatism then dominating science in the Anglo-Saxon world. After the Second World War, both men further developed critical theory and were joined by their important disciple, Jürgen Habermas. In the 1960s critical theory has significantly influenced conversation within the sciences of human behavior, especially in West Germany. Discussion of critical theory among both critics and defenders has, meanwhile, revealed it to have more in common with the "critical rationalism" of Popper and Albert than could have been supposed upon its initial formulation. Nevertheless, the two theories differ with respect to their methods, categories, goals, and analyses of the present situation.

On the one hand, critical theory's "interest in the maturity and fulfillment of man is understandable . . . since, from within the entire philosophical tradition, these are the only ideas over which we have some command."[17] On the other hand, for critical theory as for critical rationalism, the ideas of human maturity and enlightenment threaten to become vague and indeterminate—empty utopian rhetoric. The critical recollection and transformation of philosophical traditions which should prevent this from happening is, therefore, an integral part of critical theory, even in terms of its own self-understanding. While Horkheimer, Adorno, and Habermas go about this task of recovery in different ways, all three undertake to reconstruct philosophically the process of human emancipation. To arrive at their reconstructions, they critically appropriate elements of the Judaeo-Christian and philosophical heritage and dialectically reinterpret Enlightenment traditions which furthered the process of rational emancipation: e.g., Kant and Hegel, Marx and Freud. At the same time they examine those Enlightenment countercurrents which led to the dissolution of the process of human emancipation in modern times.

Critical theory deems necessary a thoughtful recollection and adaptation of the traditions of the German Enlightenment in order that the meaning of freedom and the substance of progress become clear. Scientific reason is increasingly instrumental, society increasingly governed by technology, and individuals increasingly powerless and susceptible to manipulation. Emancipation through revolution and reform is ever more difficult. In this situation, it is imperative to insist that freedom from the tyranny of nature and the domination of man over man means more than sociotechnical progress or blind revolutionary action; similarly that progress means more than constantly increasing needs, production, and consumption. Hence, when critical theory recalls the thinking of the German

Enlightenment, it does so not for historical reasons, but in the interest of human liberation. Not by mere chance has critical theory entered into a fundamental conversation with this tradition—especially with Kant, Hegel, Marx, and Freud. Its aim is to develop further their models by incorporating new scientific discoveries and societal experiences so as to make them productive for practical philosophy.

The debate about critical theory and, above all, the attempt to give further formulation to the original thought of Adorno and Horkheimer, have focused some fundamental questions. Critical theory has not taken up these questions, nor can it satisfactorily do so within its theoretical premises. Let us elaborate.

1. In Adorno's reconstruction of the process of human emancipation the concept "totality" plays a constitutive role. Adorno employs it not only to describe what mankind has been, but also to project what mankind will be. "If man remains caught up in a totality that he himself has constructed, then (as Kafka points out) no progress has taken place; and yet man can only conceive progress by employing the idea of 'totality'." Thus, for Adorno "totality" is both a descriptive and a critical category. "The very dependence of progress upon totality is actually an impediment to progress."[18] Adorno negatively delineates his understanding of totality and dialectical method in his confrontation with positivism and, more generally, with that objectified consciousness which, in his opinion, has come to dominate the social and scientific enterprise. For Adorno, totality means neither (1) "the absence of contradiction" which is implicit in a "logical analysis of the idea of totality," nor (2) "verifiability according to some criterion of facticity," nor (3) "statements that positivistic systems theories might bring together in a consistent logical continuum merely through the selection of the most general categories possible."[19] That objectified consciousness now dominant in science and society, owing to the commercial principles of modern capitalism, is itself, in Adorno's view, "a moment in the totality of the objectified world."[20] Dialectical thinking should expose this form of consciousness as alienated and unreal. "The more a society steers toward totality," remarks Adorno, "the greater will be its tendency to dissociation."[21] Therefore, he who wishes to understand the inauthenticity of contemporary society

must employ the idea of totality dialectically. "In other words, he must resist the temptation to ontologize the idea of social totality or to make it into a first principle of being."[22]

Since Adorno cannot clarify his concept of totality directly, using the methods of objectified consciousness, he necessarily has recourse to another point of departure which he finds in the German Enlightenment tradition, particularly in Kant and Hegel. However, Adorno cannot really connect up with this tradition because certain Kantian and Hegelian contentions about totality hold for him untenable religious and metaphysical implications which must be consigned to the past. After the elimination of these implications, Kant's concept of totality turns, for Adorno, into a mere ideal anticipation forever out of reach. Hegel's philosophy becomes a philosophy of identity, an inconsistent immanentization of the absolute, and a relapse into pre-Kantian ontology (which can only deal with individuals as examples of general types).

In spite of all this, Adorno contends in his *Negative Dialectic* that he can explain his own dialectical method and notion of totality by means of a reciprocal correction of Kantian and Hegelian philosophy. "Kant is great," Adorno says, "not because he clings tenaciously to the unity of reason in spite of his inconsistent use of it as a theoretical causal-mechanical model of nature, on the one hand, and as an aesthetic-rational synthesis of nature, on the other. Nor is Kant great because he attributes the discriminations of reason strictly to the self-delimitation of scientific thought in its attempt to control nature. A metaphysical interpretation of Kant would not impute a latent ontology to him. Rather, it would have to read the structure of his whole thought as a dialectic of enlightenment. Hegel, the dialectician par excellence, does not preserve this dialectic because he sacrifices delimitation and plurality to the unity of reason, and thus slips into a mythical totality which he understands as the absolute idea of reconciliation."[23] Hegel's greatness, in comparison to Kant's, consists for Adorno in the fact that Hegel, like his successor Marx, attempts to understand totality more radically in relation to history and society.

If Adorno wants to sharpen his thinking in relation to positivism, pragmatism, and the technologically controlled world, he must do this through determinate negations—just as in his attempt to go beyond Kant and Hegel. With regard to generalizing constructs, he remarks that "it seems almost whimsical to want to set out world history using categories such as Freedom and Justice, as Hegel has done."[24] "The scorn with which these authors have always spoken about economics, i.e., about the power that they didn't possess, is a scorn directed against the weak. Hence, in their scorn, they have identified, quite against their will, with the oppression that they themselves wished to undo."[25]

Since Adorno can only evolve his idea of totality out of specific negations, his thinking gets entangled in the dilemma that certainly afflicts modern society, the dilemma from which he is unable to extricate himself: the dissociation of reflection and action. The "whole" (totality) described by Adorno is always the unreal; his dialectic is always negative; his critique is always "total." "In that it is dialectical, theory (including Marxist theory) must be immanent, even if this means that it must finally negate the entire sphere in which it itself operates."[26] The end result is that the theoretical enterprise falls into insuperable difficulties. We can grant, with Adorno, that the basic context of thinking, which classical German philosophy calls "totality," must be constitutive for any practical philosophy which seeks to be more than the formulation of technical methods of action. Adorno's concept of totality, however, lacks a satisfactory connection with what was, what is, and what should be.

We can also grant, with Adorno, that mankind is not totally ensnared in this noxious age, but is dependent more than ever before, in the face of undeniable antihistorical tendencies, on the critical recollection and transformation of traditions in order to preserve human freedom. However, Adorno's negative dialectic is not a method with which one can rationally designate specific content mediated by history and worthy of preservation. Nor can it ascertain and convey definite foundations and ethical norms for individual, social, and political activity. By its very nature, Adorno's negative dialectic is not a procedure for rationally testing traditions, but rather a method for condemning them. All the appeals of negative dialectic to the traditions of metaphysics, classical theory, aesthetics, and religion can be but mere conjurings. Recollection (even critical recollection) that is unable to affirm for itself what it remembers cannot be made fruitful for the present. While Adorno, with this idea, wants to reflect and criticize the "whole" as "untruth," i.e., as an alienated and objectified world scheme, he runs into the same problem as Hegel, whose concept of totality he criticizes. Hegel's concept also leaves unreconciled and outside of itself "the unresolved polarities under which our age suffers,"[27] for Hegel wanted to present the "whole" as "truth" scientifically unfolded. "How the present age is to find its way out of its unresolved polarities," remarks Hegel, "is left up to it."[28] Adorno's interpretation of all problems of the bourgeois society as "late capitalism" and "the consequence of the commercial principle" is not sufficiently differentiated to do justice to the economy of developed industrial societies. For him to speak of "the increasing importance of instrumental reason in scientific planning and technical administration" hardly suffices to explain all the social and political power conflicts in capitalist and socialist societies, let alone in the Third World. A "total critique" and rejection of the existing order, i.e., an "apotheosis of negativity itself," only makes one blind to the tensions and "unresolved polarities" in the various institutions under which "our age suffers" and also blinds one to alternative courses of action and concrete reforms that are possible today. A "total critique" of all existing authorities, powers, and institutions in the name of a utopia beyond them all can lead to skeptical indifference or blind activism, as recent experience shows. This outcome is possible because a *total* critique is unable to formulate any definite criteria for analysis and reform within the system. In fact, both indifference and sheer activism, precisely because they change nothing, actually reinforce those forms of authority, power, and institutions which today ought to be changed.

A theory which must be satisfied with "loyalty to the commandment against all images, even images that were not prohibited in the original commandment," cannot be made fruitful for practice. Nor can such a theory appeal to the great tradition of negative philosophy and theology, because its method of negation begins with religious, philosophical, ethical, and social assumptions that are not acceptable today. A philosophy seeking in our time to articulate the inexpressible becomes (in Adorno's case and others) an expression of hope that is actually hopeless unless it accepts a reason for hope, whether a specific tradition or some principle of hope. A philosophy that thinks it must explode the supposed oppression of a totally controlled world becomes an appeal to a spontaneity that can no longer be counted on. So, Adorno says that "we need men who are alive in order to change hardened conditions, but the hardened conditions have themselves entered so deeply into men today, stifling their lives and individuality, that they appear scarcely capable of that spontaneity on which everything depends."[29] But this very thing that Adorno regards as "real thinking" turns out to be exactly that for which he criticizes Heidegger. Adorno's "real thinking" can, in "the midst of universal suffering" and dread, only express itself metaphorically and aesthetically, as for example: "This limitless endurance, this never extinguishable sweet impulse of the creature towards expression and light, seems itself to soften and to satisfy the force of the creative unfolding."[30]

In this dilemma philosophy threatens to become what Adorno calls "essay." An essay presents all of its ideas in such a way that they bear one another, each articulating itself in a configuration with others. By and through an essay, discrete elements set over against one another come together to form a readable whole. An essay furnishes no scaffolding or framework for its readers, but its elements crystallize themselves into a configuration through the movement of the language. Insofar as this configuration is a field of power, every mental image of the reader changes itself into a field of power."[31]

The concepts of reconciliation and redemption which accompany that of totality in classical German philosophy threaten to become, in the thought of Adorno, mere categories or ideas. Out of his experience with fascism, Stalinism, positivism, pragmatism, capitalism, and technologism, arose Adorno's belief that practical philosophy could remain philosophy only if it held firm to the traditional concept of totality. Since Adorno's concept of totality is incapable of reconciling the "unresolved polarities" under which "our age suffers," we must look for new possibilities of reconciliation—even if the philosophers themselves, today as yesterday, remain "untroubled about what will happen to the world," and "how the world will find its way out."[32]

2. The isolation of Horkheimer's and Adorno's critical theory

from scientific and social processes has become increasingly evident in the last few years, as the following two points indicate.

a. In their *Dialectic of Enlightenment*, Adorno and Horkheimer explain the decline of Enlightenment rationality and the ever-growing dominance of instrumental reason observable today by invoking that idea of controlling nature "at the cost of nature" which is present in myths and in the Enlightenment. This interpretation of myths and the Enlightenment (and, indirectly, of the decline of Enlightenment rationality and the ascendancy of instrumental reason) assumes their connection with the theological notion of the resurrection of nature, i.e., with the idea of a fixed and natural development of mankind which can be overcome in the process of emancipation from the blind tyranny of nature "in and outside of human society." Now, this theological notion has, indeed, a long history, which E. Bloch in particular has outlined. However, it can no longer hold up in dialogue with the sciences: biological anthropology, ethnology, linguistics, and the natural history of behavior all tend to disconfirm it. Moreover, changes in the concept and experience of nature in modern technological society, its art, and literature, make it unlikely that freedom and emancipation can be understood by means of this theological notion. How, then, can Adorno and Horkheimer assume that this idea underlies the present decline of enlightenment and the increasing instrumentalization of reason?

b. Habermas has tried, at least until now, to terminate the isolation of critical theory from science and society by continuing the Kantian tradition in the form of an immanent criticism of the methods of the analytical and hermeneutical sciences. If this criticism is to attain its goal and not remain locked into intrascientific reflection on method or skepticism, then it must develop criteria which can be employed productively in interdisciplinary dialogue for the purpose of (1) analyzing the unresolved tensions within various institutions, and (2) discussing the factors in the alleviation of such tensions. As we shall see, Habermas has not yet satisfactorily developed such interdisciplinary criteria through his immanent methodological criticism. Moreover, his suggestions for reform of the university appear not to be based on the procedure of scientific reflection on method, nor do they appear capable of being established through such a procedure. Consequently, Habermas's theory of science seems to remain isolated from social and political action.

3. Horkheimer, Adorno, and Habermas have shown why the bourgeois subject who was once the reason for political and social progress is turning into a powerless victim of manipulation. They have also shown that, as a result, autonomy and maturity can today take shape and realize themselves, if at all, only by other means than at the beginnings of capitalist society. Furthermore, they have shown why the person-subject can no longer be understood as inwardness either in the pietistic or aesthetic sense (as in the eighteenth and nineteenth centuries), or as absolute ego or subjectivity defined by the processes of reflection (as in classical German idealism). Adorno, Habermas, and Horkheimer, among others, advance many arguments for the decline of the bourgeois subject that are of long standing, having been formulated already by Lessing, Hamann, Kant, Hegel, and Kierkegaard.

Yet in spite of the evident disappearance of the bourgeois subject, critical theory has held fast to this concept of subject. Indeed, there are weighty reasons for philosophy to retain or redefine this concept, as I shall later show. Nonetheless, we cannot surreptitiously do away with the immense *caveat* that the use of this notion presents for the representatives of critical theory. The following reasons can be given for this *caveat*. As pointed out by Adorno and somewhat differently by Marcuse, the subject can often express himself only aesthetically because of the prevalence of false consciousness. Horkheimer tries to ground the subject in a "Wholly Other" (religiously understood) and attempts this in view of the impending decay of culture and morality in a scientifically and technically manipulated world. Habermas, rather than evading this difficulty, attempts to construct an accurate definition of the subject (i.e., individual) in conversation with linguistic and social theories. Yet it remains unclear to what extent his present academic interest still implies adherence to the concept of subject as transmitted through specific traditions of the Enlightenment and as unintelligible apart from that mediation.

4. Habermas has recently been trying to put an end to the isolation of critical theory from science, society, and politics by turning, in his reconstruction of mankind's movement toward emancipation, not to the German Enlightenment tradition of Kant

and Hegel, Marx and Freud, as much as to linguistic and social theories coming out of the Anglo-Saxon world. He begins with the thesis that modern science and technology is a "new ideology" that threatens our real interest in maintaining the intersubjectivity of human understanding, and, as well, our attempt to establish a human communication that is liberated from oppression. From this starting point Habermas then attempts to conserve and secure "these two fundamental conditions of our cultural existence: namely, the intersubjectivity of human understanding and free human communication. Technical consciousness allows our real concern for these values to diminish in the face of its own preoccupation with expanding our technical capabilities. The intellectual reflection that challenges "technological ideology" must, therefore, get underneath the historically constituted class interests and expose the set of values which all men share."[33]

The pivotal idea in Habermas's reconstruction of the process of human emancipation is that of "interests." This concept is used in constantly changing ways to mean: (1) an "intellectual interest" that leads thought to analyze and criticize definite historical positions, and (2) a "practical interest" in emancipation that gives rise to universal historical processes, whose presence can be demonstrated within specific historical positions. Habermas's continually changing use of the term "interests" leaves open a number of questions, a few of which we should consider.

Habermas in his historical and systematic writings uses the concept "intellectual interest" to analyze and criticize two distinct epistemological concerns: the instrumental-empirical-analytical (directed toward the scientific control of nature), and the communicative-hermeneutical (directed toward an understanding of modes of communication and behavior in an attempt to clarify the self-understanding of the acting subject). Habermas holds that these two epistemological interests are themselves related to different systems of action, which he contrasts as follows: goal-oriented action versus symbolically mediated interaction, work versus speech, technology versus communication.

Here we must introduce the following questions. What can an interpretation of philosophical traditions through the notion of "interests" accomplish and what are its limitations? How does Habermas ground these intellectual interests if not anthropologically

(Gehlen) or philosophically (the German Enlightenment)? In what sense are both of the structures of action described above mutually exclusive alternatives, as Habermas assumes? And, most importantly, what do these structures of knowledge and action imply for an anlysis and critique of concrete economic, social, and political patterns of behavior in a world controlled and characterized by the conflict of many diverse power groups?

In addition, the interpretation of interest as interest in emancipation opens up another series of questions. In view of the actual development of science and technology, Habermas can no longer simply identify the process of emancipation with scientific and technological progress, as did Bacon and Condorcet. Nor can Habermas offer precise criteria to differentiate those interests that stimulate progress and are, therefore, human from those that stand in its way and are, thus, inhuman (as did the later Hegel through his theory of absolute knowledge, and Marx through his critique of political economy). Consequently, the interest in emancipation threatens to become "pure criticism" whose dead-end character has already been demonstrated by the left-wing Hegelians, especially Marx. To avoid the impasse of "pure criticism" Habermas attempts to explain the goals of the process of emancipation (e.g., maturity, autonomy, and free communication) in an a priori way, i.e., not on the basis of history, but on the basis of the "structure of language."

This procedure is unsatisfactory for a number of reasons. The ideals derived from the "structure of language" threaten to turn into weak and nebulous regulative ideas because of the manifold experiences of negativity and evil in their individual, social, and political dimensions. Moreover, the ideals tend to become impotent and incommunicable because of practical, nonlinguistic forces and factors that science describes and explains. Habermas rightly perceives that in a post-Darwinian and post-Freudian age the goals of the emancipation process can no longer be fully explained by and rooted in a "structure of order" that belongs to a presocial and prehistorical, natural state of man. Can the interest in maturity be "a priori deduced" from the "structure of language," as Habermas contends, in spite of the dwindling of traditions and the development of posthistorical structures of reality? Is there anything in the structure of language itself that requires an interest in the public-social conditions of maturity, autonomy, and free communication?

Habermas's method of basing interest in emancipation on the "structure of language" is unsatisfactory for yet other reasons. First of all, an idealistic view of language is involved in his procedure, i.e., a view of language as creating rather than describing its object. No theory of language deduces interest in emancipation from the "structure of language" as Habermas does. This is done neither by the philosophy of ordinary language that describes the popular linguistic usage of expressions, nor by Chomsky's linguistics (that, as he puts it, looks for "innate ideas") nor by the philosophical hermeneutics of Gadamer who, in dependence on Heidegger, inquires into the logos of rational speech. Rather, an analysis of language in our controlled world illuminates other patterns and necessary conditions of communications that rely not on the autonomy and freedom of subjects in the area of communications but rather on their suppression and manipulation.

Finally, the analysis of political language demonstrates how communication can be distorted and obscured. It reveals a motive to dominate others, which is independent of language. The desire to liberate cannot be deduced from the patterns of an a priori logic of language and communications. Even academic discussion can take place according to the standards of free communication only if its participants are capable and prepared. Up until now Habermas has been unable, at least building on his idealistic view of language, to develop clear, a priori criteria that would make it possible to distinguish serious talk about the desire for emancipation from mere chatter about it. In any event, this difficulty should now be discussed more precisely in connection with the logic of language and communications—which will, furthermore, reveal how very fluid the boundaries between critical theory and the logic of language-and-communications become in Habermas's work.

IV. *The Unresolved Problems within the "Logic of Language-and-Communications" and "Systems Theories"*

Many of those previously "self-evident" assumptions of science and society now no longer appear as self-evident with respect to the advance of human enlightenment. In industrial societies those scientific theories that create the impression that the modern emancipation process has come to a standstill are today gaining influence in the social and behavioral sciences. For them the controversies between positivists and dialecticians, Christians and Marxists, have grown virtually pointless.

The consequences of such "scientific fashions" are especially visible in French structuralism which, perceiving itself to be both a scientific method and a political task, sets out to attack both history and humanism. It intends, as Foucault has said, not to adapt traditional interpretations, but "to render the very idea of man superfluous in both research and reflection. . . . To 'save' man or to 'rediscover the humanity of man' is the goal of all these interdisciplinary babblings that, for example, attempt to reconcile Marx and Teilhard de Chardin, etc. Such undertakings exemplify that which, through the ages, has condemned intellectual work to sterility. The task assigned to us is to free ourselves from humanism once and for all. In this sense, then, our project is political—for all the governments of both the East and the West sell their dirty wares under the flag of 'humanism.' We must denounce all this mystification."[34]

That structuralism which understands itself as a "political task" assaults history on the grounds that the thinking and acting of contemporary man is completely determined by the posthistorical structures of science and technology into which he is now fully integrated. The effort now being put forth by some of our generation consists not in opposing science and technology for the sake of man, but in demonstrating that our thought, life, and behavior, down to the most ordinary activities, belong to the same scheme of organization and depend on the same categories as the scientific-technological world itself."[35] Analogies between preindividualistic and postindividualistic societies should legitimate a procedure that wishes to rediscover a system of structures which, in principle, precedes human thought and existence—à la Rousseau. But unlike those thinkers who, interested in enlarging freedom, consistently sought criteria for furthering enlightenment in the distinction between "prehistorical" and "historical" societies, structuralists are not concerned with differences between "cold" and "hot" societies.

Rather, they are interested in those quasi-ontological, presubjective, and ahistorical structures that all societies have in common. Structuralism's attack on history and humanity has frequently been criticized for its methodological faddism—and it need not be given more space here.

At the present time in industrial societies, an attempt is being made to get beyond the debate between positivists and dialecticians. This effort is directed toward discovering, in dependence upon theoretical developments in the English-speaking world, categories useful for describing and criticizing social and political processes. Two sets of scientific theories engaged in this work may be characterized as "language-and-communications theories" and "sociological and political systems theories." The residual problems of these theories can also be taken up to demonstrate why practical philosophy must speak about a continuing process of freedom and enlightenment.

The "logic of language-and-communication" assumes that "the answers supplied by authority, whether from the past (tradition) or from the present (teachers, ideals, political institutions) are no longer effective."[36] Moreover, it supposes that philosophy is today ruled by a "confusion of tongues" wherein "positions and opinions are hopelessly defended against one another."[37] As the way out of this impasse, the logic of language-and-communications, drawing on the tradition of Kantian transcendental philosophy, suggests that the philosophy of language become the fundamental philosophical concern. It offers this suggestion even though similar attempts along these lines in recent times have not been convincing. Lorenz proposes that the philosophy of language should, "without falling back upon either ordinary language or the practice of the traditional sciences,"[38] produce those a priori "rules for disciplined dialogue" which are taken for granted in our "preunderstanding of the world and of ourselves" even prior to reflection and research. In searching, via the philosophy of language, for "a linguistic structure that precedes both formal logic and mathematics,"[39] the logic of language-and-communications hopes to discover in the communication process itself the rules that make possible a rational, free and non-tendentious communication. It hopes to find the invariable conditions of "precise and controlled dialogue, conditions that perfectly fulfill the requirements of rational behavior."[40]

The procedure used by the logic of language-and-communications implies two presuppositions that are subject to dispute. The first is the belief that logic can establish invariant and universal "rules of disciplined dialogue," and that these rules are recognizable as generally applying to disciplined dialogue and behavior by every participant in dialogue, irrespective of time and place. Regardless of who utters the proposition, of where or when it is uttered, the justification of the intended activity remains, with respect to its validity, unaffected by variation of circumstances."[41]

The second presupposition of the logic of language-and-communications is the implicit analogy between speaking and acting, linguistic forms and behavioral forms, linguistic action and individual and societal action. Lorenz affirms: "The substantiation of statements is a rational and therefore formally good action."[42] Similarly, Kamlah and Lorenzen write: "The work we have begun here in reflecting on the possibility of meaningful speaking is a reflection on our actions as well, and is, therefore, a practical reflection."[43] Nevertheless, whereas practical philosophy in the European tradition (with the help of Platonic dialectic) sought to achieve a consensus about the means to the good and happy life under concrete social conditions, the logic of language-and-communications is concerned only with one kind of activity—linguistic activity. Rather than setting out to establish a foundation for the activities of individuals and groups in the traditional sense, it occupies itself with establishing a foundation for general utterances about human action.

To repeat, neither of these presuppositions of the logic of language and communications is self-evident. Invariant rules of a rational, free, and nontendentious dialogue cannot be rationally established by logic and mathematics or by metaphysics and metaethics. The multiplicity of logics, mathematics, and metatheories —and, in particular, the internal critique of their methods—has shown that "the decision to proceed rationally can never itself be rationally justified."[44] Lorenzen himself concedes that "not even mathematics, the most rigorous of the sciences, can establish itself without moral argumentation."[45] The decision to discuss ethical and political questions in a rational way is not a "natural capacity of man," but is dependent on definite assumptions mediated by the

European tradition—whether we admit it or not. Apart from the meaning provided by this tradition, the concepts "rational" and "free" are vacuous ideas. The "fundamental decision in favor of rational argumentation in the moral realm" and, thus, in favor of maturity and freedom, cannot, as Lenk has shown, be rationally established or justified by a metaethics or even a metametaethics.[46]

The decisive question that the logic of speech-and-communication has yet to answer satisfactorily is whether or not criteria to provide a rational basis for political decisions and to resolve conflicts within various institutions are, in fact, derivable from the construction of an ideal language or from the invariable rules of "a precisely regulated dialogue." The question is whether the decision-making processes in the United Nations, in business, in the universities, in churches, and so forth will become more lucid and rational when carried on in conformity with invariably valid rules for dialogue. To ask these questions is in no way to prefer blind decisionism as opposed to rational argumentation. Quite the contrary. Such questions wish merely to make clear that social and political decisions are dependent on factors and interests not given a priori within the structure of language. They wish simply to show that interdisciplinary conversation conducted according to "invariant rules of dialogue" (which, for this reason, must bracket out certain unresolved historical and material problems under discussion in individual disciplines) threatens to become pseudoconversation. Whoever pleads for rational discussion should not begin by eliminating certain divisive factors that cannot be specified by means of the invariant rules of speech. Whether this new fundamental philosophy, in looking back over 2,500 years, finds itself today for the first time in secure possession of a viable instrument for carrying out its task is an open question.

We come now to a second set of questions connected with systems theory.

Discussion of the advantages and disadvantages of systems theory for the analysis of social and political processes has recently become more intense in Germany and the English-speaking world. With regard to these discussions, we must now delineate that unresolved set of problems to which a practical philosophy must address itself for the purpose of clarifying the presuppositions and problems of the modern enlightenment movement. The investigations under-taken by systems theory are not without presuppositions; but these only begin to emerge when the activities of science, society, politics, and commerce are scientifically planned and technically adminis-tered. At such a time it is no longer possible to proffer an adequate description and explanation of the necessary processes of decision and control in terms of traditional common-sense ideals or hardened liberal and socialist ideologies, explanations that are actually pseudoscientific justifications of revolutionary action. So, for example, Niklaus Luhmann, in his critique of Max Weber's basic concepts, has sought to show that "the simple notions belonging to our everyday orientations to social life (e.g., end and means, command and obedience) are not useful tools for ordering our thought and behavior."[47] Furthermore, Luhmann insists that the rationality of individual behavior is different from that of social and political processes in the technological world.

Naturally, systems thinkers describe and account for social and political processes with the concept "systems." This concept, de-veloped originally in information-theory and biology, must now be differentiated in such a way as to be descriptive of social and political processes. Along these lines Luhmann writes: "Systems are production units that are sensitive and open to their environments and that assimilate and adjust to feedback. Systems regulate themselves by processes of information and learning, maintaining themselves against the threat of their environment through a process of interaction with it."[48]

Both external criticism and internal discussions of social systems theory have focused until now on three lingering problems: (1) whether systems analyses have any heuristic value; (2) whether they have an adequate theoretical basis; (3) whether their con-sequences for the behavior of individuals and societies have been sufficiently thought out.

1. The heuristic value of cybernetic analyses of actual processing and use of information in industrial societies together with analyses of concrete historical developments (e.g., the decision made by the government of Israel during the 1956 Sinai campaign) is very slight. Cybernetic models, in spite of recent methodological re-finements, are not yet capable of illuminating all the factors neces-

sary for analyzing concrete social and political phenomena. Systems theories will be able to mirror reality only when and if individuals and social groups are totally integrated into a self-regulating system. Since this has not yet come about in either the West and East or the Third World, the use of systems theory in the practical sciences today only contributes to "widening the gap between theoretical commitments and empirical observations."[49]

2. Systems theory cannot compensate for its lack of heuristic usefulness by engaging in metatheoretical reflection, however it may try. According to Naschold, systems analysis "posits a new frame of reference, a novel metatheory that advances a claim to universality." An examination of its past attempts to establish metatheoretical foundations has led to the following conclusion: "Systems theory still lacks that comprehensive, consistent, and satisfactory concept of value priorities which is the necessary presupposition of decision-making. Whether such a scale of value priorities can be attained by means of the methods it has used to date is very uncertain."[50] The most fundamental judgment of metatheory is itself not free from being contradicted, a fact that brings us to our third point.

3. The basic objection to sociological and political systems theories is that they have not reflected on their consequences for practical behavior. Another objection concerns their supposed neutrality with respect to values. Sociological and political systems theories are occupied with developing criteria that serve the self-maintenance and self-regulation of a system whose processes of decision and control are complex. As Luhmann says, "the preservation of a system in the midst of a threatening environment is increasingly becoming the center of scientific interest."[51] However, this interest is ultimately, as Narr rightly suggests, "a kind of 'System Darwinism' in which every means is justified if it serves the goal of system survival."[52] But the mere "maintenance of the system in a difficult environment" is not an adequate criterion when certain kinds of social and political decisions are unavoidable, e.g., the means to avoid war, to secure peace, to overcome hunger, oppression, and injustice, to reduce tensions among different political and economic blocks. "The thesis of Deutsch and Senghass that self-regulation and social-individual emancipation converge"[53] is still only an hypothesis. The employment of systems theory in industrial

societies is no argument for its ideological neutrality. In such societies, there are, assuredly, special areas where processes of decision and control can be more suitably handled with cybernetic methods. Nevertheless, social and political goals and priorities cannot be determined by these methods. If Daniel Bell and Noam Chomsky are right in their contention that war rather than peace is responsible for governmental introduction of planning and technocratic methods, then this is not a matter of "indifference" for the social and political systems theory that claims to be "value free."

The unresolved problems in scientific theories which contend that the modern emancipation process is at a standstill argue against the truth of these theories. The fact that unresolved problems exist demonstrates that we should not speak of a "standstill" but rather of an "impasse" to which the enlightenment movement has come. We turn now to this dilemma.

V. *Three Presuppositions of the Modern Process of Freedom and Enlightenment*

If practical philosophy is to deal with the unresolved problems in contemporary theories of science and society (without regressing to a pre-Kantian viewpoint), it must take up at least three presuppositions or problems. In a time when freedom and enlightenment are being threatened, whoever takes a stand for the promotion of these two values can certainly offer more grounds for his decision than often appears to be the case. By supporting his stand with argumentation, he lessens the arbitrary character of his decision— even though, in the last analysis, he cannot offer an absolutely compelling scientific justification for his commitment to these values. In the end, his commitment to freedom and enlightenment remains disputable because it is a rational and moral decision; and, moreover, it is not only disputable by skeptics and cynics. The acceptance of the Enlightenment philosophy that I am advocating need not be compelling or plausible to everyone. This philosophy is not the only tradition on which to establish and secure contemporary freedom. There is no philosophy that can prove to itself or to others its "presuppositionlessness." This much, at least, the critical dialogue with scientific and social theories has demonstrated.

German philosophy discussed the three presuppositions or prob-

lems of the modern enlightenment movement in conjunction with
various sets of concepts: (1) subject, subjectivity, and person;
(2) negation and evil in their individual, social, and political
aspects—i.e., alienation, separation, and negative identity; (3) liberated humanity, the highest good, ultimate purpose, totality, and
reconciliation. It is perfectly obvious that we cannot here explore
the parameters and full meanings of these concepts in German
classical philosophy.

A practical philosophy desirous of making a contribution to the
resolution of certain contemporary problems finds itself hard
pressed to develop an appropriate conceptuality. This is more than
a mere semantic difficulty, as recent hermeneutical discussions have
shown. The meaning of the essential concepts is no longer obvious
and unambiguous, owing to the history of their employment and
their contemporary use. However, to relinquish such concepts
would mean to abandon the problems bound up with them. Whoever uses the concepts "freedom" and "peace" must at the same
time stipulate what he does not mean by them, because they have
been so misused. But, unless he wants to surrender the set of relations traditionally designated by these ideas, he cannot renounce
the ideas themselves. New concepts that unambiguously express the
web of relations designated by "freedom" and "peace" have not
yet been developed. Specifically, these relations cannot be articulated through the conceptuality of certain linguistic and systems
theories. Nor does the coining of new philosophical vocabulary make
these concepts more plausible in the public and political order.
Typically, Heidegger's new linguistic creations have about them
an esoteric and eccentric aura that conveys how problematic such
a procedure is. This not only applies to the concepts "freedom" and
"peace," but also to other ideas.

While the development of an appropriate philosophical conceptuality is surely more difficult today than in Kant's time, there
is still no reason for contemporary philosophy to proceed otherwise than as Kant himself suggested.

> Despite the great wealth of our language, the thinker often finds him-
> self at a loss for the expression which exactly fits his concept, and
> for want of which he is unable to be really intelligible to others or
> even to himself. To coin new words is to advance a claim to legisla-

tion in language that seldom succeeds; and before we have recourse to this desperate expedient it is advisable to look about in a dead and learned language to see whether the concept and its appropriate expression are not already there provided. Even if the old-time usage of a term should have become somewhat uncertain through the carelessness of those who introduced it, it is always better to hold fast to the meaning which distinctively belongs to it (even though it remains doubtful whether it was originally used in precisely this sense) than to defeat our purpose by making ourselves unintelligible.[54]

1. In order to clarify the presuppositions or problems of the modern enlightenment movement, practical philosophy must in some way speak about what classical German philosophy designated by the concepts "subject," "subjectivity," and "person." Its conversation with scientific and social theories has shown that to understand man as subject, or subjectivity, or person is to understand him as a being who is rooted in nature and natural history, but not determined by a complex of instincts and drives. It is to understand him as a being who is socialized through language, work, interaction, and culture. But up to the present time, no society has existed which regards man as a self-creating subject. What classical German philosophy intends by "man" is the being who has become "subject" or "subjectivity" or "person" in a world shaped by the Greco-Roman and Judaeo-Christian traditions as well as by the industrial and social revolutions of the eighteenth and nineteenth centuries. According to this philosophy, man is only man when and if he recognizes himself as a subject and is, at the same time, acknowledged as a subject by society, law, the state, art, religion, and philosophy.

Wherever man does not know himself as an end, wherever he continues to use other persons as mere means, wherever laws, society, and the state still do not safeguard the rights of men as men, and where the family and religion in their rules and structures do not respect man as subject—there, according to classical German philosophy, one cannot speak about the realization of man as a subject, nor, subsequently, about freedom and enlightenment. Kant and Hegel see the fulfillment of human emancipation as demanding not only increased consciousness of freedom, but also a real freedom present and experienced in institutions. Overcoming the presocial and prehistorical natural condition of man (to prevent regression into this state) belongs to the attainment of freedom. "Man can be compelled to abandon his natural condition: *statu naturali*." For Hegel, realization of freedom implies the overcoming of "unhistorical history" distinguished by conflict among social groups and a cycle of events in which man still does not know himself and is not yet recognized as subject. (Hegel assumed such an "unhistorical history" to exist in Africa and Asia.)

Classical German philosophy has also held subjectivity to be "a source of both progress and corruption." As Hegel formulated the matter: if the subject who contains subjectivity in himself isolates (and must isolate) himself from the world as it has been historically formed, then the freedom which is intended in the very concept of "the subject" is threatened. The subject who, containing subjectivity in himself, believes out of skepticism, resignation or egotism, that he can renounce the historical development of freedom and enlightenment, destroys the very conditions of his own realization (in art, religion, philosophy, ethics, and politics). For Hegel, the realization of man as subject takes place through artistic experience and literary education, which presumes man's openness to art and poetry. The artistic-literary medium was and still is "the most universal teacher of the human race, for teaching and learning are knowing and experiencing what is. Stars, plants, animals do not know and experience the law of their being. But man alone begins to exist in relation to the law of his being when he knows what he himself is and what surrounds him. A man must know the powers which drive and direct him, and it is poetry, in its primary substantial form, which gives his knowledge."[55] But Hegel also holds that the realization of man as subject requires his formation by Christianity and his openness to this shaping force. "Philosophy and faith," he says, "have the word of God as their sole foundation and the restoration of fallen nature (i.e., the redemption of nature) as their goal. . . . Both are supernatural in so far as they raise man above fallen nature, something which cannot be accomplished by nature on its own. Both are natural as well, in so far as they have the restoration of true nature as their outcome."[56]

The subject who only perceives himself as aesthetic or spiritual inwardness was condemned by classical German philosophy as an empty immediacy. The absolute I who believes himself able to constitute himself as an absolute I through a process of private reflection was dismissed by German philosophy as an abstract product of thought. German philosophy regarded the revolutionary bourgeois subject who understood freedom as emancipation from the past not as universal, but as particular; not as free, but as unfree. Many of the contemporary arguments predicting the decline and fall of the subject already have a long history.

Regardless of the preceding, contemporary philosophy cannot, in designating the human subject as a presupposition of the enlightenment process, adopt the very same starting point as German classical philosophy. For one thing, the religious and philosophical traditions of Europe are no longer asserted with the same force as formerly. Moreover, efforts to establish a basis for understanding what is here called the "subject" have already begun in non-European societies and in non-Christian religion. These efforts have proceeded through conversation with the European tradition and through internal transformation of the various non-European traditions. The plurality and diversity of traditions within the single world that is coming into being means that philosophy can no longer operate in terms of a pure European heritage (as did classical German philosophy).

The nineteenth and twentieth centuries have unearthed other new conditions responsible for a change in man's consciousness as subject and necessary for the realization and preservation of man as subject. The economic development of industrial societies has illustrated how, today, the forms of economic behavior created at the beginning of the industrial age serve not only the liberation of man from the tyranny of nature, but also his suppression and manipulation. Social tensions and revolutions have witnessed the necessity of intra- and extragovernmental legal structures regulated by laws and contracts in order to protect man as subject. These same tensions and revolutions have also witnessed the tendency of legal structures to become unjust when effective control is lacking to prevent their being corruptly employed by powerful social groups as instruments of suppression and exploitation. Both Marxism and psychoanalysis have demonstrated that the appeal to reason, to freedom, and to the maturity of human subjects remains ineffectual if the conditions of society prevent subjects from being rational, free, and mature.

Once philosophy deems the understanding of man as subject to be a precondition for the modern advance of enlightenment, it can hereby appeal to the behavioral sciences and to a responsive public—in spite of all arguments to the contrary. The behavioral sciences are, themselves, seeking to redefine what has been traditionally designated by the concepts "subject," "subjectivity," and "person." This redefinition is imperative if they wish to speak without cynicism about the destiny of man in a postindividual society, about his total integration into old and unchangeable institutions (Gehlen), or his total adaption to new social and political systems. Even in social and political life the concepts "subject," "subjectivity," and "persons" carry more than a pejorative meaning. They indicate not simply what man's primitive integration into archaic institutions has destroyed (Gehlen), or what has been lost to man's primordial mimesis—i.e., recollecting thought (Heidegger)—or even what was and is historically specific about the bourgeois individual. The assumptions articulated by existentialism and personalism are certainly necessary, but not sufficient, for a criticism of the one-dimensional structures of man and society. These assumptions are implicit in their descriptions of the I-thou relation, their discussion of intersubjectivity, and their developed antithesis between the I-thou and the it-world relationships. For these reasons, and because of the escalating manipulation, impotence, despair, and loneliness of individuals in a technologically controlled society, practical philosophy is obliged to protect and preserve what has been traditionally designated by the concepts "subject," "subjectivity," and "person."

2. In order to speak concretely about the human subject, practical philosophy must also discuss what negativity and evil are in their individual, social, and political dimensions. In other words, it must discuss social and political evil as alienation, separation, and nonidentity. Dialogue with scientific and social theories has made this clear. Not only Horkheimer and Adorno, but also Karl Deutsch explores the various manifestations of evil

in society and politics. While the problematic of evil and negativity today is undoubtedly multifaceted, ambiguous, and hard to circumscribe, its circumscription is not impossible. The individual is subject not only to sicknesses and death, but to the various forms of suffering that individuals and groups inflict upon one another. He experiences these even if he cannot and will not give expression to them in the language of suffering connected with a traditional form of religious and aesthetic piety.

Many theories for interpreting evil supplied by European theological and philosophical traditions are no longer persuasive because they underestimate these evil forces, rendering them innocuous. This criticism applies to some extent to the interpretation of evil as nonbeing, to the hypostatization of evil as a supernatural being or metaphysical principle, and to the inadequate differentiation between natural calamities and moral evils. It has some truth for any superficial treatment of the problem of theodicy, and for most interpretations of "original sin" and concupiscence. However, philosophy, on this account, has no right to keep quiet about the manifold forms of negativity and evil. It should not, in the name of some perennial legitimating concept, eliminate this idea of evil from the scope of its considerations as something purely private and incidental. Nor should it denigrate the concept of evil as an unsystematic and nonfunctional concept. If linguistic and analytical philosophy rejects as unscholarly a discussion of the problem of negativity and evil, banishing to the realm of art and literature those who take it seriously, then this is symptomatic of the impasse in analytical and linguistic philosophy! It is even an argument against it!

Although many proposals developed by German classical philosophy to explain evil are not very convincing, the phenomenon they are trying to explicate can still be pinpointed today. Kant's hypothesized corruption of our basic moral stance or principle by an intellectual act that betrays it, preceding every empirical deed, is no longer plausible—at least to those who know how problematic the Kantian distinction between the empirical and the rational ego is. Nevertheless, men can, even now, experience themselves as living in a world rendered ambiguous by a multiplicity of modes of being that are both human and inhuman. They experience this world as something not explicable by their individual actions nor transformable by them to allow men to live in peace with themselves and others. The various hypotheses of classical German philosophy predicating, as the origins of historical evil, man's necessary and unavoidable fall into "sin" from a natural state appear unscientific in our times. Nonetheless, today's men neither experience nor judge the countless kinds of oppression, injustice, violence, and crime as "natural." Even if many traditional interpretations of evil are superficial from the psychological and sociological point of view, or function to legitimate illegitimate power structures, oppression, injustice, violence, and crime remain what these concepts mean in ordinary language. Even if the newer ideas of "alienation" and "separation" have picked up additional meanings from their variagated usage (i.e., by Marxists and existentialists, theologians and nontheologians), the phenomenon of negativity and evil is still with us. New concepts can grow indefinite, laden with diverse meanings, just as the old ones have, e.g., as the concepts in the traditional catalog of deadly sins (lust, envy, pride, sloth, etc.) have become vague. Auschwitz and Hiroshima, fascism and Stalinism are, in spite of the theories of Lorenz, more than one can explain by using the method of analogy from the animal world. They are more than "misdirected aggression." As Kant said, war remains "the flagellation of the human race," and remains so even if the powers that precipitate it and the weapons employed have become more anonymous. In view of the growing hunger in the world and the suppression of men and peoples, the Stoic idea of "eternal return" is unconsoling and downright cynical. Despair and indignation about man's suppression and indifference to it is surely, as Adorno argues, more moral than "that abominable presumption of the dogma of original sin that the depravity of human nature justifies the domination of men by other men, i.e., that radical evil justifies evil."[57] Philosophy must also address itself to the problem of evil in its individual and political dimensions if it wishes to discuss emancipation and enlightenment in a concrete and credible way.

In coming to terms with the problem of evil we must begin by criticizing modern philosophy's doubting or depreciating the reality of evil, even if evil is depreciated in the name of enlightenment. Philosophy must begin by illuminating the dialectic of understanding evil. In his criticism of inadequate theological and philosophical theories about man's fall into sin, Rousseau tried to formulate social reasons to explain human unfreedom and inequality. But this image of man as good by nature and only evil because of changeable social relations is, Kant reminds us, "simply a congenial assumption of moralists from Seneca to Rousseau," a "heroic idea that has found acceptance only among philosophers and particularly, in our time, among pedagogues."[58] Eighteenth-century attempts at rational theodicy, i.e., attempts to reconcile evil in the world with the idea of a good God, utilized the image of the legal process. For instance, Leibniz spoke of the "tribunal of reason" and Kant of the "court of reason." While these tries at theodicy admittedly aimed at liberating human reason, they are illegitimate not only on theological but also on philosophical grounds. Lessing, Hamann, Kant, and Kierkegaard all concur in finding them invalid. Opposing modern attempts to demythologize theological and philosophical interpretations of evil, Kierkegaard declared long ago that "no age has been more suited to the creation of myths about reason than ours, for our age creates myths in its very willingness to uproot them all." Theodicy's twentieth-century revival by neoscholasticism has not succeeded any better. Every rational theodicy is refuted by more than the suffering of innocent children, as Dostoevsky and Camus have shown. Granted, the theories to account for evil provided by Feuerbach, Marx, Nietzsche, Freud, and Lorenz have certainly played a necessary corrective function. Nevertheless, these attempts to develop a "morality without guilt" for the sake of mankind's freedom have often resulted in an undermining of the reality of evil in personal, social, and political existence.

If practical philosophy is to take up the problem of negativity and evil in these various dimensions, it must look for such interpretations of evil as can be made fruitful in the struggle against injustice. Philosophy must not remain smugly satisfied with a denunciation of evil and a moralistic rejection of a totally controlled world. Rather, it should look for ways and means to overcome evil or, at least, to reduce it. As Noam Chomsky says:

> Anger, outrage, confessions of overwhelming guilt may be good therapy; they can also become a barrier to effective action, which can always be made to seem incommensurable with the enormity of

the crime. Nothing is easier than to adopt a new form of self-indulgence, no less debilitating than the old apathy. The danger is substantial. It is hardly a novel insight that confession of guilt can be institutionalized as a technique for evading what must be done. It is even possible to achieve a feeling of satisfaction by contemplating one's evil nature. . . . We must guard against the kind of revolutionary rhetoric that would have had Karl Marx burn down the British Museum because it was merely part of a repressive society. It would be criminal to overlook the serious flaws and inadequacies in our institutions, or to fail to utilize the substantial degree of freedom that most of us enjoy, within the framework of these flawed institutions, to modify them or even replace them by a better social order.[59]

No longer able to contruct credible explanations of evil in terms of a single factor, (e.g., the moral factor of choosing the wrong), practical philosophy must approach this problem in conversation with other disciplines, with society and politics. In this way it can avoid abstract talk about the emancipation process.

3. Discussion with theories of science and society, as well as the unresolved problems of personal and political life have shown why practical philosophy cannot evade those questions concerning the ideal goals of human behavior. Certainly it can no longer speak of a liberated mankind, a highest good, the goal of history, the kingdom of God, totality, and redemption in the same way as did classical German philosophy. Owing to their positivist conception of science, the early Carnap and Wittgenstein looked upon questions about ethical goals of action as meaningless. For Foucault's structuralism, for particular sociological and political systems theories, and for the logic of language-and-communications, questions concerning the final goal of action are unscientific, purely historical, and private. The experience of the twentieth century has prompted Adorno to call for a radical opposing of images in philosophy, believing that if, in the midst of universal gloom, philosophy paints a picture of an intact world, it only veils the gloom, rendering it temporarily innocuous.

The unresolved problems in Adorno's philosophy and in other theories of science and society illuminate those questions with which classical German philosophy sought to deal. Even today we cannot boast of an enlightened age. The condition of emancipation historically achieved is not yet the state of sufficiently realized freedom. While the history of the nineteenth and twentieth centuries has been a series of efforts to institutionalize the freedom and rights of the human subject, these efforts have never been decisively successful, and on occasion have even been abortive. Evidencing this failure are the unresolved tensions and conflicts in Western and Easten societies and in the Third World, and, more particularly, the many-sided threats to freedom and human rights in industrially developed and underdeveloped societies. These numerous manifestations of negativity and evil have revealed the modern enlightenment movement to be neither completed nor at a standstill.

If practical philosophy today wishes to say something plausible and compelling about the goals of human action, then it is hereby directed to interdisciplinary discussion. Ernest monologues and deductions from absolute nonhistorical truths can no longer expect to be universally received. Two examples will serve to illustrate what practical philosophy can still say about the ideals of human action.

a. Institutionalization of the freedom and rights of human subjects is an Enlightenment problem which, up till now, has not been accorded enough attention in theories of science and society, critical theory included. This problem occupies the center of discussion within the practical sciences and various institutions (e.g., the family, the university, the church, and the state), and holds sway equally among defenders and critics of the Enlightenment.. The increasingly rapid pace of change in technology, the economy, society, and politics has meant that traditional institutions are being questioned by more and more people. There is a resulting increase in the tensions with which the consciousness and lives of their participants are fraught, many being capable of only a partial identification with the institutions in which they live.

For classical German philosophy, enlightenment does not imply the release of the human spirit from bondage to institutions. Rather, it means the critique and reform of institutions that do not adequately acknowledge the freedom and rights of the subject, and the creation of new institutions that generate and protect this freedom and these rights. For Kant and Hegel, the standard for the institutionalization of human dignity was the "mature judgment of an age that no longer allows itself to be held back by pseudo-knowledge."[60] As Hegel said: "The criterion of validity today should be insight and reason over against power, habit and tradition."[61]

Kant was convinced that effective social and legal institutions could be created to safeguard human freedom and rights. This protection would involve legal arrangements and treaties within and among states, according to a rationally intelligible local, national, and international civil code. Hegel was persuaded that in the state (as an ethical whole) the family, civil society, social classes, corporations, and churches could all be so coordinated with one another that they would serve to protect human freedom and rights. Evidence is constantly accumulating to support the necessity of other institutions for the defense of freedom and the realization of human rights. The civil society that administers justice (as Kant conceived it) is a necessary, but not sufficient, guarantee for the fulfillment and preservation of freedom and human rights. Hegel's "state of realized freedom" offered no conditions for a freedom adequately attained by all.

A practical philosophy that today wishes to say something plausible and compelling about institutions must not only enter into interdisciplinary dialogue, but must also engage the concrete conditions of various societies. For example, in a technologically controlled world the state and its decision-making functions are neither an ethical universe distinguishable from the society nor an instrument of domination by a special class. Moreover, the state never "fades away"—not even a socialist state! In Europe and America, parliamentary democracy was and still is an institution that protects freedom and the fundamental rights formulated in its constitutions. Despite failures, it can accomplish this owing to the economic, liberal, and religious traditions that exist in the Western world. For other societies, however, paraliamentary democracy need not be the best political institution for the preservation of human rights. It is still an open question as to what kinds of political institutions socialist and Third World societies will be able to develop, given their circumstances. Where poverty prevails and "at a time when not even the seeds of new institutions exist,

‍‍‍

let alone the moral and political consciousness that could lead to a basic modification of social life,"[62] other institutionalizations of human freedom and rights are necessary than those which presuppose prosperity.

Kant could still allege that the "improvement of the political constitution in our part of the world would probably in the future result in its furnishing every other part of the world with norms."[63] On the other hand, the obvious problems of today and the foreseeable future suggest that in societies ordered by different economic, social, and spiritual traditions there are needed various ways to institutionalize freedom and maintain human rights. Tension and conflict in numerous and varied societies prove that the reform and transformation of institutions cannot be accomplished according to a single model. The "democratization" of political institutions and churches is something quite different from the creation of new institutions to ground freedom and safeguard human rights. Educational institutions and economic enterprises are more readily changed than the fundamental laws of the modern state. According to the intentions of their founders, these basic laws should persist as legal norms for a relatively long time, somewhat contrary to the insistence of natural law theorists that they should be forever unchangeable. What the enlightenment movement today requires is a new understanding and reform of institutions so that they will serve the realization of freedom and human rights and win the approval of men.

b. The critical recollection and adaptation of the Christian tradition had decisive significance for classical German philosophy in its discussion of the goals of human activity. For example, Lessing in his remark that the final goal of mankind (i.e., a liberation in which man does good for the sake of good) is not yet "either completely hidden or completely revealed," is relying on a schemata borrowed from Christian theology, in spite of his critique of theology. Kant, in speaking of the "last things" in which a worthy man ought to hope, is consciously falling back on the central teachings of Christianity, in spite of his critique of the Church. Hegel, in his attempt to understand reconciliation, is dependent upon the Christian doctrine of reconciliation, in spite of his critique of Christianity.

Now, assuredly, contemporary practical philosophy can no

longer have recourse to Christian traditions in the way that classical German philosophy did. In our single universe, there is a plurality of traditions, and the increasingly acute problem is to mediate among them. Since every science and every society has undergone changes since the eighteenth century, the attempt of classical German philosophy to recall and transform certain teachings of the Christian tradition might today seem not at all enlightened, but even ideological. Then, as now, there are some who hope to achieve the final victory of emancipation through a radical break with Christianity. However, with the multidimensional threats to human freedom taking on a new clarity, the fear that theology might threaten the autonomy, self-understanding, and "legitimacy of modern times" is not nearly so pronounced today as is the fear that theology might offer no convincing contribution to the self-understanding of man and the securing of his threatened freedom.

The presuppositions of philosophy prevent it from saying what the presuppositions of theology and the Church impel them to say: namely, something about the ultimate goals of mankind. Nevertheless, if philosophy is to contribute to the modern emancipation process, it should on principle be open to "an offer that is foreign to it, that does not arise in its domain, but that is nonetheless adequately attested to."[64] Philosophy should be open to this offer even if "it cannot construct from it a philosophical concept."[65] Speaking out of its own presuppositions, philosophy can, perhaps, affirm the following: if the churches do not involve themselves in the movement toward enlightenment because of a concern to protect their traditions, then they become more and more individualized and sectarian. And if they believe they can preserve their identities in an inwardness that is not reconcilable with the present, then they become more and more otherworldly. And if they become otherworldly, then they can no longer relate to the very biblical confessions and ecclesial teachings which they themselves profess.

If, on the other hand, the churches and theologians abandon their specific presuppositions and accommodate themselves superficially to the secularized world and its trends, then they lose their own identity and the continuity of their traditions without even gaining credibility in the world's eyes. Churches and theologies which furnish plausible information about the goals of human action in an attempt to contribute to the realization of these goals are obliged to respect the conditions of the modern enlightenment process. Finally, if practical philosophy is to take up the unresolved problems in theories of science and society with the goal of furthering human freedom, it must not only talk about subjects, negativity, and evil, but also about the goals of human activity developed by science and society.

NOTES

1. Ludwig Wittgenstein, *Tractatus logico-philosophicus*, 6:42.
2. Rudolf Carnap, *Logische Syntax der Sprache*, (1934), p. 204.
3. Karl Popper, *Die offene Gesellschaft und ihre Feinde*, (1958), 2:293.
4. Popper, *Logik der Forschung*, (1966), vol. 14.
5. Hans Albert, "Plaedoyer für Kritische Rationalismus," *Das 198. Jahrzehnt. Eine Team-Prognose für 1970–1980*, ed C. Grosner, et al., (1969), p. 298.
6. Popper, *Logik der Forschung*, vol. 16.
7. Ibid., vols. 22–23.
8. Albert, op. cit., pp. 286, 289.
9. Popper, "Die Logik der Sozialwissenschaften," *Der Positivismusstreit in der deutschen Soziologie*, (1969), p. 114.
10. Albert, *Traktat über kritische Vernunft* (1968), p. 67.
11. Popper, *Logik der Forschung*, p. 225.
12. Ibid., pp. 69–70.
13. Albert, "Plaedoyer," pp. 298–299.
14. Popper, "Die Logik der Sozialwissenschaften," p. 121.
15. Ibid., p. 113.
16. Albert, "Plaedoyer," p. 292.
17. Jürgen Habermas, *Technik und Wissenschaft als "Ideologie,"* (1968), p. 163.
18. Theodore Adorno, *Stichworte. Kritische Modelle* (1969), 2:30–31.
19. Adorno, "Einleitung," *Der Positivismusstreit*, p. 19.
20. Adorno, *Negative Dialektik* (1966), p. 100.

21. Ibid., p. 337.
22. Adorno, "Einleitung," p. 48.
23. Adorno, *Stichworte. Kritische Modelle*, 2:39–40.
24. Max Horkheimer and Adorno, *Dialektik der Aufklärung*, (1969), p. 234.
25. Ibid., p. 236.
26. Adorno, *Negative Dialektik*, p. 195.
27. G. W. F. Hegel, *Vorlesungen über die Philosophie der Religion*, ed. G. Lasson, I:1, p. 311.
28. Ibid., II: 2, p. 231.
29. Adorno, "Gesellschaft," *Evangelisches Staatslexikon* (1967), p. 637.
30. Horkheimer and Adorno, op. cit., pp. 236–237.
31. Adorno, *Noten zur Literatur* (1958), 1:30.
32. Hegel, op. cit., II:2, p. 231.
33. Habermas, op. cit., p. 91.
34. Quoted in Schiwy, *Der französische Strukturalismus*, (1969), pp. 205–206.
35. Ibid., p. 207.
36. K. Lorenz, "Die Ethik der Logik," *Das Problem der Sprache*, ed. H. G. Gadamer, p. 81.
37. W. Kamlah and P. Lorenzen, *Logische Propaedeutik oder Vorschule der vernuenftigen Redens*, (1967), p. 13.
38. Lorenz, op. cit., p. 86.
39. Kamlah and Lorenzen, op. cit., pp. 11, 14–15.
40. Lorenz, op. cit., p. 82.
41. Ibid., pp. 82–84.
42. Ibid., pp. 83–84.
43. Kamlah and Lorenzen, op. cit., p. 234.
44. Lenk, *Der "Ordinary Language Approach*," p. 201.
45. Lorenzen, *Methodisches Denken*, (1968), p. 161.
46. Lenk, op. cit., pp. 201, 205.
47. Niklaus Luhmann, "Zweck-Herrschaft-System. Grundbegriffe und Praemissen Max Webers," *Der Staat* 3 (1964): 129–158, 146–147.
48. Ibid., pp. 147–148.
49. Naschold, *Systemsteuerung*, (1969), p. 165.
50. Ibid., pp. 162, 46.
51. Luhmann, op. cit., p. 148.
52. Narr, *Theoriebegriffe und Systemtheorie*, p. 176.
53. Naschold, loc. cit.
54. Immanuel Kant, *Critique of Pure Reason*, trans. N. K. Smith, (New York: St. Martin's, 1929), p. 309.

55. Hegel, *Aesthetik*, ed. F. Bassenge, (1955), p. 879.

56. Hegel, *Berliner Schriften 1818–1831*, ed. J. Hoffmeister, (1956), p. 324.

57. Adorno, *Stichworte. Kritische Modelle*, 2:40.

58. Kant, *Werke*, ed. Ernst Cassirer, 6:158.

59. Noam Chomsky, *American Power and the New Mandarins* (New York: Pantheon, 1969), p. 17ff.

60. Kant, *Werke*, 3:7.

61. Hegel, *Rechtsphilosophie*, prop. 316.

62. Chomsky, op. cit., p. 17.

63. Kant, *Werke*, 4:165.

64. Ibid., 5:131.

65. Ibid., 6:411.

JOHANN BAPTIST METZ

5. Prophetic Authority

Translated by David Kelly and Henry Vander Goot
Introduction by David Kelly

Introduction

Johann Baptist Metz was a relatively unknown German diocesan priest in the early 1960s when the Second Vatican Council opened in Rome. In the intervening decade his contributions to theological discussion have made him one of the central figures in European Catholic theology. Many consider him to be the logical successor to Karl Rahner in the field of systematic theology.

Metz is the originator of the term "political theology" in contemporary usage, and is identified with this theological school. It should be noted that the term "politics" does not denote to the German what it denotes to the North American. In the German mind politics is a human concern involving principles that relate to the nature of man and the goals of society. Hence, the German emphasizes principles rather than pragmatics in relation to political policies. For the German, politics is not first and foremost bargaining or electioneering. Rather, it is the science of the structural principles of social order. With this in mind, we can understand Metz's definition of political theology. He writes "The theology of the world is neither a purely objectivistic theology of the cosmos nor a purely transcendental theology of the person and existence. It is a political theology. The creative-militant hope behind it is related essentially to the world as society and to the forces within it that change the world."[1]

The immediate context of Metz's essay is an anticipated pastoral synod of Catholic Bishops in Germany (first convened in 1971). But the issues Metz deals with are hardly limited to this setting. It is true that German theological usage cannot be translated into the North American idiom without some attempt at nuance and at recognizing the difference of philosophical and political-social milieu. Nevertheless, it is also quite clear that the practical problems of authority in the German situation are similar to our own. The wider context of Metz's essay is the crisis of authority in the modern world.

There is another reason why Metz's essay has immediate relevance. His stated aim is not to solve particular practical problems relating to authority and freedom. Rather, he intends to develop an explicitly theoretical basis for the investigation of such problems. He deals with issues that underlie the practical political situation. These issues are common to Europe and North America. They constitute, *mutatis mutandis,* the common base for parallel crises in the churches today. North Americans are frequently interested in the problem of authority because of its implications for mandatory celibacy, episcopal collegiality, rights of the laity, etc. These issues are indeed important. But Metz's essay takes us into a wider perspective on the problem of authority in light of the positive critique brought to bear on it by the spirit of the Enlightenment.

It is in this connection that the term "authority-crisis" appears in Metz's article. The concept is especially familar to Roman Catholics. The immediate context is Vatican II. Renewed interest in biblical studies, new developments in ecclesiology, and reforms of the liturgy symbolize many of the council's changes. What would once simply have been accepted on the authority of the Vatican is now apt to become the subject of controversy in private and public.

At Vatican II the Roman Catholic Church began its renewal by reviewing its own self-understanding; and it did this in a way unprecedented in recent history. The Church's authority in principle and in fact has become a central issue in contemporary Roman Catholic theology and institutional theory. For Metz, however, the uneasiness created by internal reform is not the basic cause of the crisis of authority in the Roman Catholic Church. In his essay Metz shows how the real roots lie deeper, especially in the ongoing isolation of church authority from the spirit of the Enlightenment.

The material principle of the early Enlightenment was its criticism of tradition and external authority. With the loss of traditional community came the loss of traditional authority. However, between the time of the demise of absolute monarchs and the rise of the modern nation-state, new centers of unprecedented power were created in the name of the people. Accordingly, authority becomes synonymous with total political power.

A clear example of this fateful identification of authority and total political power is the socialist "democracy" of the Third Reich. Twentieth-century criticism of modern political authoritarianism has focused on the Nazi perversion of power. Before, during and after the Second World War the question of political leadership and its relationship to authority was raised with new vigor.

One direction taken by concern over this question was studies of the authoritarian personality. The trend-setting study in the area was Adorno *et al, The Authoritarian Personality,* a massive research project undertaken by the Frankfurt School of Social Research. Given the shocking experience of Nazi brutality, it seemed imperative to identify the origins and dimensions of the personality type whose need for authority obviated the necessity for consideration of right and wrong, even in a matter so massive as the extermination of a race. Erich Fromm also contributed to the investigation of this problem in his *Escape from Freedom,* which examines the sociocultural origins of the authority-dependent person.

In earlier studies on the authoritarian personality interest focused on such factors as fascism, ethnocentricism, dogmatism, and racism. Eventually, however, investigation generalized to such personality factors as open- versus closed-mindedness, flexibility versus rigidity, and simple versus complex cognitive or conceptual styles. Metz draws upon this pattern of contrasts in his own distinction between "ecclesiastical" and "sectarian" in the final section of his essay.

Metz's discussion of authority is only one piece in his larger project of developing a "political theology." For example, his contribution to *Diskussion zur politischen Theorie* (ed. H. Peukert; Mainz, 1969) develops the distinction between "state" and "society." "I believe," says Metz, "this historical distinction is important if democracy is not to succumb to apolitical forms of social order."

Most recently, Metz is publishing a theological interpretation of society that stresses the social function of faith as "dangerous memory." For example, in his essay on *Erinnerung* (memory) in the *Handbuch philosophischer Grundbegriffe* (Munich, 1974) Metz argues that a theologically serious concern with the Enlightenment must not simply reproduce the Enlightenment's dichotomy between authority and freedom or between tradition and reason. Rather, it must show how true authority presupposes and sustains true freedom; and it must show how memory does not merely transmit the past, but also opens the future.

Metz himself has suggested that a portion of his *Concilium* Congress lecture, "The Dangerous Memory of the Freedom of Jesus," be added as the final section of his essay in this volume. Those who do not know his political theology are advised to turn to "The Dangerous Memory of the Freedom of Jesus" before reading his discussion of authority. It suggests the larger context in which his essay should be interpreted.

Metz's own interpretation of the way in which his contribution to this volume is related to that of the American authors is as follows: "The notion of 'memory' I have developed offers a theological category capable of criticizing any attempt apolitically to suppress religious pluralism. At the same time, through its intrinsic relation to the 'eschatological proviso' (cf. pp. 19-21), it offers an historical—rather than an ahistorical—context for understanding religious transcendence. Hence my development of 'memory' is relevant both to Richardson's discussion of religious transcendence as well as open to Bryant's reflections on the critical significance of eternal life and the Trinity with regard to the relation of religion and political society."

Prophetic Authority

I. *Introduction*

Any theology that intends to be critically responsible for the Christian faith and its transmission cannot ignore "social" and "practical" issues.[2] Furthermore, genuine theological reflection does not permit itself to be isolated from the problems of the public good, the law, the present status of freedom, etc. Moreover, theology must recognize a fact that has become especially clear since the Enlightenment and the post-Idealist critique of religion: namely, the Church is indeed always active as a political power, even before it adopts any explicit political position, and thus prior to any debate about the basis of this or that actual political attitude. For this reason theology considers the Church's assumption of its own neutrality as either naive or deceptive. Through the development of a *practical-critical*[3] hermeneutic, theology seeks to prevent the Church from identifying itself uncritically with particular political ideologies. Accordingly, theology strives to prevent the Church from degenerating into a purely political religion, or at least from functioning as such. Understood in this way reflection on the political horizon in theology would be a form of *practical-critical* ecclesiology. This applies both in view of the present configuration of church and society, and in view of the traditional structures and patterns of life of the Christian faith. The issue of ecclesiastical authority in the context of the challenge of the modern history of freedom[4] (an issue to which we now turn) should illustrate this.

In dealing with this theme we are taking for granted that there can be such a thing as church authority and that it can have a basis in theology. Hence we will not deal directly with the theological justification of church authority. In addition, we will touch only peripherally on questions that concern the relationship of church authority, scriptural authority, and the authority of the self-revealing God. However weighty these questions may be, their treatment here would exceed the scope of this essay. Besides, they can be given an adequate theological treatment only if they are dealt with in the context of a theological theory of the Church's present situation.

Nor will we discuss the distinction between church authority and church officials. This essay does not address itself immediately to the frequently discussed questions concerning changes in the concrete modes of exercising church offices; e.g., such issues as methods of electing church officials, new collegial forms of cooperation among ecclesiastical offices, a possible limit on terms of office, etc. The investigation of the theme "church authority" as it is presented here tries to get at more fundamental theological relationships, though admittedly with the practical-critical purpose of providing a basis for revitalizing the idea and exercise of church authority. Besides being an essential part of theology in its theoretical mode this "practical purpose" also serves as warning to those theologies that resist ecclesiastical change or renewal. Such theology is guided by an impulse to justify existing ways of life and practices in the Church. Whether this theological interest is a priori "more churchly" than testing the spirits within the Church itself (as is tacitly assumed) is questionable on good theological grounds. To show why this is so one need only consider the motives of those extraecclesiastical groups and institutions (political, economic, and ideological) that have a keen interest in keeping the structures, morality, and practices of the Church exactly as they are!

Finally, we can only deal peripherally with the "liberal" distinction between the Church and Christianity (or between ecclesial tradition and Christian tradition)—an issue of importance for a comprehensive understanding of the theme "church authority and the history of freedom." No one, in taking the distinction seriously, should allow himself to understand it in such a way that Christianity could be summarily disassociated from the institution and authority of the Church; for in this way Christianity would lose its identity and finally be reduced to a superfluous religious reflection of the actual social, political, and cultural developments of modern times. A Christian theology that would attempt such a disassociation of Christianity from the institutional Church would, in my opinion, become merely an ideological theology, resembling the theology of those who oppose all renewal. However, such an ideological theology, instead of being an apologetic for the ecclesiastical history of Christianity, would be an apologetic for the history of modern times and the understanding of freedom accompanying it.

II. *Church Authority and the Challenge of the Modern History of Freedom*

"Crisis of authority": this phrase is on everyone's lips, even within the Church. For the Catholic Church the crisis is frequently linked to Vatican II and often explained in terms of the continuing unrest generated by subsequent reforms. Such an explanation is too superficial, however, for the roots and theological-historical conditions of this crisis obviously lie much deeper and must be taken into account. A definite and helpful orientation can be derived from a consideration of these roots and conditions of the crisis of authority. Such reflection can at least break through the clichés in which the present controversy is all too often frozen and can help us avoid the one-sidedness and fruitless impasses that constantly arise out of the crass opposition of authority and freedom.

The roots of the crisis of authority lie, in my opinion, in an isolation of the Church's practical understanding of authority from the contemporary history of freedom, an isolation which, naturally, has serious consequences for the Church's identity and mission. This crisis of authority appears to be caused mainly by the fact that the legacy of the modern world and the Enlightenment, which has been suppressed and ignored in the Church, is now penetrating into the very heart of the Church with its "principle of freedom." A serious and unequivocal acceptance of this challenge could and should be the substance of an attempt at church renewal. Renewal must thus, not be an opportunistic accommodation to the world and petty intraecclesiastical changes that are mere alibis for genuine reform. Furthermore, renewal must be accompanied by a healthy dose of skepticism about easy victory in a confrontation with the modern history of freedom and enlightenment. Instead of aiming at abolishing church authority or functionalizing it in a pragmatic way, the goal of renewal should be (1) a decisive victory over the isolation of the Church's understanding of authority from the modern history of freedom, and (2) the subsequent development of a vital authoritative witness. Only an elimination of this isolation can block the advance of merely passive accommodation and do away with the impression that ecclesiastical reforms always originate less from the free initiative of the spirit and from inner forces of renewal than from anonymous pressure and coercion from the "outside." The issue here is not whether the Church should create a cheap modernity and presence in the world for itself. That would be to slide uncritically into the prevailing illusions of a one-dimensional now. The issue at stake here is rather that of the historical identity and mission of the Church itself.

The thesis that the Church's practical understanding of authority is isolated from the modern history of freedom requires a fundamental clarification, and that in two respects. First, it must be noted that this proposition gives utterance to a theological thesis about the contemporary world as it is conditioned by the modern age and the Enlightenment. Understood as a theological thesis, it cannot be criticized or contradicted by a mere enumeration of historical facts but only by the proffering of an alternative theory of the modern age and the Enlightenment. Any one who seeks to refute this argument by disputing the usefulness or even the scientific possibility of such a theological interpretation of the modern situation must at least be aware of the consequences of his objection.

On the one hand he is throwing doubt on the very possibility of a modern theology, and, thus, of theology in general; for the reduction of theology to biblical theology (or biblical hermeneutics) is equivalent to disputing the present possibility of theology. Biblical theology cannot (for reasons that are intrinsic to it) relinquish the theological characterization and analysis of the history of modern times without uncritically minimizing the historical remoteness of the unrepeatable situation of the biblical witness, or without dogmatically asserting a doctrine of biblical infallibility.

On the other hand anyone who places in doubt the legitimacy of a theory of the modern age and the Enlightenment reduces, in an antihermeneutical fashion, the work of historical science and historical criticism to a new historical positivism. That is, he eliminates the problem of the motive and purpose of a critical interpretation of history from the subject matter of historical science itself. A critical-philosophical theory of the modern age actually accompanies every descriptive history of the age. Certainly each theological interpretation of the modern age can and must confront these theories directly.

Second, the idea of the modern history of freedom that is contained in our theological thesis must be protected from misunderstandings. This idea should pinpoint the historical place which the theme of freedom is achieving in the modern world, thus making it impossible to regard and treat "freedom" merely as one theme or one problem among others. The continuing modern course of emancipation does not just focus upon man qua man, that is on the free human subjectivity as universal master over nature. It also involves the concrete institutionalization of this freedom in religious, social, political, and economic structures. To undertake a theological discussion of this history of freedom is not to deny that freedom was a motif in earlier epochs of European Christian tradition. Nor is this theological interpretation an uncritical approval of the actual course of the modern process of freedom and enlightenment, which would be something like a theological canonization of the one-dimensional notion of linear progress. Such a theological optimism is under the spell of the idea of a supposed discursive (as opposed to dialectical), step-by-step advance of an ever-expanding freedom. Furthermore, such a theological interpretation would be a theological canonization of an historically insensitive cliché about the Enlightenment and the world come of age in which the conflicts and negative aspects of the freedom already attained are nicely glossed over. What my thesis intends and demands is an eventual victory over the isolation of the Church and its concrete structure and public stance from the fundamental impulses of the modern history of freedom.

On the whole the Catholic Church in its institutional manifestations has related only negatively to the modern history of freedom. The creative and critical power of assimilation that characterized earlier periods of the Church has been missing. The Church has stood repeatedly on the side of resentment and reservation, and even of pure opposition and, consequently, has developed few specifically modern traditions. The "high ages" of the Catholic Church within the modern period did not primarily derive their self-understanding from the tradition of this period, but instead looked back to earlier times. The "ages of the Church" were counterreformation and counterrevolution, counterenlightenment, and restoration, and finally romanticism and neoscholasticism and their ecclesiastical and theological legacy in our own day. The presence of existentialism in contemporary Catholic theology does not contradict this; for, through its theological reduction of history to the historicity of personal existence, existentialism kept the concrete history of the modern period and the Enlightenment (the arena of the mediation and vindication of biblical traditions) hidden from the view of theology and the Church. In this way existentialism relieved theology and the Church from dealing with the challenges of the modern age.

For one more example from the contemporary theological situation one need only look at Kant's reception by Catholic systematic theology; that is revealing enough. To be sure, Kant's formal transcendentalism has been discussed and at least partially digested. But Kant's valid teachings on the primacy of practical reason, where the problematic of freedom can be found explicitly, have not been taken seriously.

It is in the new theology, however, which serves large sections of the Church's membership, that the dangerous consequences arising from the isolation of the Church from the modern history of freedom appear most clearly in the form of a certain schizophrenia. On the one hand, among official ecclesiastical representatives the newer theology is defined by a choice for the new process of freedom and enlightenment. It emphasizes the fact that Christian impulses are carried and developed within this history of freedom, and tries to develop a positive theological view of the historical process of secularization. On the other hand, the creative and critical assimilation of the process of freedom and enlightenment generated no traditions on which to base these new theological reflections.

In my opinion this schizophrenia is also present in a large part of today's church community. In its historical, social-political, and even in its religious self-understanding, this community is not reactionary, though reaction characterizes the historical and publicly visible stance of the Church. The situation is intensified by the fact that the concrete manifestations and practices of church authority come under the sphere of influence of social traditions that have developed in reaction to the modern history of freedom and enlightenment. It is surely true that the Church rejected French traditionalism in its dogmatic form, especially because of its defamation of reason. However, the self-understanding of ecclesiastical authority that is actually operative in the Church, especially in its Machiavellian view of sovereignty, exhibits very dangerous parallels to the political theories of sovereignty, authority, and structure contained in French traditionalism. This has created, or at least intensified, what I would regard as the growing danger of church authority becoming impersonal, formal, and bewildering.

Church authority has functioned too much as a power in itself, far removed both from the faith that it publicly confesses (a faith that in fact always begets freedom) and from the concrete history of faith in the church community. In short, church authority functioned too absolutistically, with the result that "church history" could be understood and described more or less as pure "papal history." By contrast, in the practice of the early Church, ecclesiastical authorities much less frequently issued dogmatic decisions from an isolated "above." The decision appeared not so much as a starting point as the result of a comprehensive process of the teaching and living of the entire Church. In recent centuries, however, the exercise of church authority has come to depend less on the teaching and life of the whole Church than on sophisticated ecclesiastical public relations. Though we are neither able nor expected to agree with the often-cited image of the Church in Dostoevsky's *Grand Inquisitor*, we must, nevertheless, always ask ourselves whether the modern exercise of church authority may not sometimes give rise to the startling impression of a religion that is no longer believed and that is, hence, preoccupied with survival alone. Obviously, anyone who is concerned about church renewal will always have to pay attention to such an impression and its latent implications.

The germinal problem in today's crisis of authority in the Church does not appear to me to be the simple fact that the Church has authority or that it has a representative authority of witness. Rather, it seems to lie, though not exclusively, in the fact that the practical self-understanding of church authority has also developed in isolation from and in opposition to the modern development of freedom. In my judgment the deeper roots of the latent schisms and conflicts in the Church lie here. These schisms weaken the power of identifying with the Church, and, according to Freud, when community identification breaks down, panic breaks out.

There were voices in the recent council which gave some hope for a solution to the problem. A definite "spirit of freedom" was in evidence—an ecclesiastical desire to build up new traditions, which in the long run is the only way old traditions can remain alive. This process will succeed only if the Church's development does not fall behind the pace begun by the council. For theology this means first of all that it must overcome the schizophrenia which now characterizes it. It must become "more honest" and abandon its merely abstract approval of the modern development of freedom, so that it can help pave the way for those changes that are significant for the Church, Christendom, and theology.

From what has been said thus far it should be perfectly clear that coming to terms with the challenge of the Enlightenment does not mean simply a stereotyped repetition of the classical Enlightenment position and its illusions. The task of church renewal is often glibly accused of this and consequently denounced, while the problems actually presented by the Enlightenment are once more suppressed. The following will show that the problem of authority and freedom no longer represents an irreconcilable antithesis for us, as it did in the Enlightenment. I have already observed that the Enlightenment critique of institutions has today acquired a completely new variation. The primary issue is no longer whether or not a critical freedom is possible within or even in opposition to existing institutions. Rather, the primary problem is the very crisis of freedom itself in its noninstitutional form and the connected question of the possible institutionalization of this critical freedom. Similarly, the following will show that today's growing problem of freedom and authority is in no way limited to the Enlightenment criticism of heteronomous sources of authority that curtail freedom. Rather, the problem deals directly with the question of an authority that could make freedom possible and could bear witness to it.

2. Up to this point I have spoken exclusively of the situation in the Catholic Church. It might seem that the problem as I have characterized it does indeed apply exclusively to the Catholic Church and not to the Protestant churches. But this is misleading in my opinion. With respect to the issue of freedom and authority the split in the Church has been disastrous enough for everyone. Isn't it true that all the churches inherited from Luther the seeds of their division, while in the long run they suppressed what was his original concern, namely the preservation of the "orthodoxy of freedom" in the one Church? And have the churches not all contributed to their growing isolation from the history of freedom, which was once considered Christian? And have not the churches so isolated themselves from this history of freedom that secular society and the state had to call their attention to the basic principle of freedom found in the Religious Peace of Augsburg and later in the Proclamation of Tolerance and Religious Freedom? Have not Protestant churches also developed reactionary trends both in their relation to the state and in the practical understanding of their own ecclesiastical structures and authorities? Does not the Protestant Church today have problems similar to those of the Catholic Church? One need only read Käsemann's *Jesus Means Freedom* and Moltmann's "Revolution of Freedom" to agree.

In my opinion this last question also applies to the traditions of liberal Protestantism and its principle of freedom. Is liberal Protestantism really the heir of Luther's *The Freedom of the Christian Man*? Has it not, rather, lost its identity by being uncritically assimilated to the liberal idea of the freedom of an enlightened bourgeoisie whose decline Marx already began to describe? And hasn't this liberalism also in its own way called into question the

true Christian idea of freedom? In this context I venture the opinion
that the Reformation, as the challenge to confront and reconcile the
Church's authority with the eschatological liberation of men in
Jesus Christ, still stands before us as an important ecumenical
challenge. Paul, who was appealed to as a basis for the Church's
division, could, as the apostle of the Christian's liberation, be a
witness for this new task.

3. We must now deal with the precise theological meaning of
what we have said up to this point, presenting a more detailed
theological defense of our remarks. I believe that the practical
self-understanding of church authority should be related to the
modern history of freedom and assimilate it. What does this mean?
But first, what does it not mean?

It does not mean that the modern history of freedom in its
scientific-technical, social, and political dimensions should be understood as *the* realization of the biblical message of freedom.
Biblical freedom is not subordinate to church authority, but rather
stands above it. Biblical freedom is not the *norma normata* but the
norma normans of the Church's witness, since it belongs to that
basis of faith which underlies every ecclesiastical claim to authority.
It is the freedom which God has set free in Jesus Christ. It is God's
eschatological process of liberation made present in Jesus' cross
and resurrection and, as such, is reducible neither to the liberal
ideal of man "coming of age" nor to the glorification of revolutionary liberation. In contrast to a Platonic idea of freedom, the
biblical message of freedom is neither indifferent nor irrelevant to
the modern history of freedom. Indeed, the biblical promise has
been the fundamental factor in the inauguration of the modern
history of freedom. Consequently, the biblical witness has the responsibility to criticize and thus redeem this modern process of
freedom and enlightenment. While the Bible speaks about the liberation of man from entanglement in sin and death through the
crucified Lord, it also talks about his liberation from all demoniza-
tions and deifications of cosmic and historical powers, that is from
every attempt to absolutize and glorify himself. It criticizes all
"absolute" forms of lordship and authority among men, that is all
forms of lordship and authority as detached from the history of
man's freedom.

The biblical message of freedom inaugurates the process of

human freedom by exorcising and relativizing these powers and lordships, handing them over to man's responsibility. "So there is nothing to boast about in anything human: Paul, Apollo, Cephas, the world, life and death, the present and the future, all are your servants; but you belong to Christ and Christ belongs to God" (I Cor. 3:21–23). There is a freedom of the Christian which the apostolic Church of Cephas and Paul serves and witnesses through this service. It is a freedom that belongs not only to the conditions and presuppositions, but to the content of the biblical message itself. Where talk about such a freedom is truncated or suppressed, there God's message remains unintelligible and inaccessible.

If the Church wishes to bear witness today to the indivisible freedom of the Christian, it cannot do so in a manner which ahistorically minimizes the distance between the present and the unrepeatable context of Jesus' message of freedom. The Church cannot simply and directly adopt biblical structures as paradigms for the form of its authority and witness to freedom, as is often facilely suggested today. Furthermore, the Church cannot simply repristinate historically earlier forms of authority that sought to proclaim freedom. Nor can it perpetuate such structures as it criticizes this modern history of freedom. For the Church's witness attains credibility only in conversation with the claims and challenges of that modern development, and in intimate relation to it alone can the Church witness the challenging redemptive story of God's liberation of man in the cross of Jesus Christ. To give such a testimony ever anew is the sole "norm" for the Church's claim and authority, the sole evidence of apostolic continuity with the gospel message itself. For only by the courageous and liberating transmission of the freedom of Christ does the visible Church continue to be the invisible Church of the spirit of Christ's freedom. In this connection Ernst Käsemann has remarked the following:

The history of Christian freedom is in this sense a way of suffering, on which the churches have to look back more in shame than pride. Jesus, in his realism and his freedom, is always in advance of his Christian people, and generally in such contrast to them that they ought to talk very much more cautiously about being "in Christ." They must on no account do so except by asking for forgiveness as sinners and claiming the justification of the unrighteous.[5]

4. But how is it possible to speak of a future for church authority in the context of the modern history of freedom and enlightenment? Do we not have to admit that the history of freedom, especially as it culminated in the Enlightenment, had as its fundamental principle the critique of all authority and the destruction of all binding traditions? Until now the Church's response has been essentially a reaction against the modern course of emancipation. Was this not the only correct and possible path for the Church to take? Surely this response alone made possible the Church's continuity, the apostolic succession of its authority, and faithfulness to its mission. What more is there to say about the need to adapt the world to the traditions of the Church? What follows is a response to this question.

Today "freedom" means just about anything you want it to mean. It can be verified in anything and reproduced in any system. In itself (i.e., as an idea) it is and has no authority capable of extension or actual verification, as the Enlightenment once thought. Freedom's authority is grounded only in those traditions in which there has been a zeal for freedom. And the future of concrete freedom depends on this zeal, handed down in traditions. Only through such zeal can a concrete knowledge of freedom be attained. This awareness cannot be derived from posthistorical forms of knowledge that prevail in modern science, for these forms of knowledge found in our new types of positivism and structuralism make the idea of freedom more and more abstract and unauthoritative.

Thus, zeal for freedom and desire for involvement in tradition no longer appear as unreconciled and irreconcilable opposites. Traditions are proving to be the conditions for a visible and concrete knowledge of freedom. Failure to recognize this was the mistake of that critique of authority and tradition which tried to establish freedom on a purely formal basis. This critique increasingly led to the anonymous tyranny of a fictitious unidimensional now, which in its nonhistorical method of desacralizing everything actually ends up concealing freedom just as much as did the religious categories of previous eras. Knowledge of freedom, even in its critical form, or, rather, particularly in its critical form, participates in tradition as recollection.

We can relate to the modern history of freedom only by a concrete and specific kind of recollection. Only this kind of concrete recollection does not once again regard history as an abstract fiction or as merely a stage on which one's own projections are played out. A concrete recollection of freedom cannot vitiate what is remembered. As a concrete recollection its remains bound to the authority of the historical witness. And precisely here—not in opposition to the modern history of freedom but within it—there is an opening onto the understanding of authority as authority which bears witness to freedom. Unlike what often happens today in ecclesiastical and theological circles, this authority need not be reduced to a purely functional authority for the purpose of organization, successful exchange of information, or mediation of divergent interests. Here in the midst and on the advancing edge of the modern history of freedom, the possibility of reconciling freedom and authority arises in a new manner.

Christian faith understood as a concrete recollection communicates the fact of freedom, celebrating itself as the liberation of man set free by God in Jesus Christ. This *memoria* of Jesus Christ is not a recollection that deceptively relieves us of the challenge of freedom's future. Nor is this memory a bourgeois alternative to hope. Rather it entails a concrete anticipation of the future of freedom. The recollection of Jesus Christ is a courageous and liberating remembrance that breaks through the limitations of a one-dimensional understanding of emancipation with its progressive destruction of real freedom. Through its challenge, the *memoria* of Jesus Christ forces us constantly to change ourselves if we do not want to lose it in the long run.

It is impossible to explain in a few words my reflections on this *memoria* as the categorial form of expression of the Christian faith and its hope of freedom. I have tried to develop this more extensively elsewhere. Nor can I elaborate further on the relationship between this image of a *memoria* that in a practical way mediates the future of freedom and history's witness to freedom. Only one more observation should be developed here. Church authority could become visible as a public witness and transmitter of this courageous and liberating recollection of freedom if in its practical self-understanding it truly accepted the challenges of the modern history of freedom. Church authority could bear witness to this

memoria if it bore concrete testimony to the gospel of reconciliation
in and alongside of the modern history of freedom, thereby making
it clear that church authority transmits its message to men who
must form their knowledge and awareness of redemption in the
context of the modern history of freedom, i.e., in the tension of
redemption and emancipation. Then the authority of its authoritative witness to freedom could be liberating—and even from both
apparent and hidden mechanisms of repression in our supposedly
emancipated society. Church authority could credibly and actively foster concrete freedom: the freedom to suffer the sufferings
of another and to hear the prophetic voice of unfamiliar sufferings
even though it always seems imposing and unbecoming to burden
the other with the negative aspect of sorrow; the freedom to grow
old, although everyone denies the reality of old age, experiencing
it as a "secret shame"; the freedom to contemplate, even though
at our deepest levels of consciousness we seem to be under the
hypnosis of work, efficiency, and planning; and, finally, the freedom
to face our own finitude and ambiguity, though our exterior suggests an ever more sound and harmonious life. Only those who are
cynical in the exercise of their power will dismiss such aspects of
freedom as sheer romanticism. Doesn't the fact of an indivisible
freedom always depend on the powerless, on those who have no
power other than the power of love and who have no allies other
than the courageous memory of an invaluable hope of freedom?
The Church must be the institutionalized desire for such a freedom,
and must represent this desire, whether this be expedient or not,
in view of the radical threats to it that have arisen in the midst of
the modern history of freedom itself. The Church's witness to that
freedom which has been set free will gain authority only if it
accommodates freedom, i.e., remains bound to the cause of love,
which by sharing suffering tries to find its own way through history.

III. *New Orientations for the Practical Self-understanding of
Church Authority and Church Consciousness*

In the preceding reflections, we have tried to gain some perspective to serve as a basis for renewal of the Church's internal practices
and structures. The renewal we envision does not arise from some

grandiose desire for reform, but from the wish to maintain continuity with the mission in which the Church believes. As important and unavoidable as the development of new models of behavior may be in such a process of reform, this does not appear to be the Church's only task. New practices remain quite sporadic. Often they only symbolize a new reality without actually creating it. In the long run these new practices are again absorbed by the "system" unless they introduce a change in the mentality that underlies the practices of the past. My observations concerning the Church's present state of awareness and the following suggestions for practical and effective notions of authority in the Church direct themselves to this deeper dimension of church renewal.

1. It is of decisive importance that many are calling into question the kind of paternal authority that still widely determines ecclesiastical and theological views on authority and obedience. Many are simply and candidly admitting that the paternal view of authority is of doubtful value. To this day we speak of the "Holy Father" and are supposed to be his "beloved sons and daughters." We speak of "Father Bishop" and of his "fatherly blessing." At the most common level of church experience, a level which is left for the most part to the pressure of reality and to the force of unavoidable confrontation, this situation is already somewhat different. For example, today we already hesitate to speak of our pastors as "fathers" of the community, although many pastors still see themselves in this way and try to interpret their office as an exercise of fatherly authority. Although such authority often remains effective precisely where it is no longer patriarchally formulated, a critical examination of and final victory over this concept of paternal authority is in my opinion of great significance in pastoral matters. This is evident in view of the continuing crisis of authority and the new relationship between the Church's exercise of authority and the modern history of freedom.

Many have called into question the appropriateness of the father image in its religious, theological, and ecclesiastical functions. The recent decline of patriarchal forms of living and, it seems, the rise of a "fatherless society" have occasioned this critical attitude. In patriarchal forms of life the child's primary experience of the father has been generalized into the public order and its relationships of lordship and authority. However important and irreplaceable this primary image of the father may be from the point of view of individual psychology (for example, as a help to the child's development and as a source of trust), it is not the most adequate category for understanding what is expressed about God the Father in Christian language. Nor is it the most unproblematic way of understanding church authority in the sense of the New Testament tradition.

It is especially because Jesus used the word that the name "father" as applied to God has become venerable for Christians. Furthermore, it will remain irreplaceable as a name for God that guarantees an eschatological hope. However, this name of God as used by Jesus cannot be interpreted psychologically. The use of the term "father" in the message of Jesus is always connected with the eschatological notion of the coming reign of God. But Jesus certainly does not understand the term "father" as a religious sanction of previous authoritarian social and political orders, or as a sanction of a patriarchal structure. Rather, Jesus understands it as the advent of the power of an unconditional love that shatters every human analogy.

In the great traditions of negative theology it is well known, if in varying degrees, that every human analogy is inadequate to express the divine. In addition, Jesus is aware of the problem when he says, "And call no one on earth 'father'; for you have only one father, and he is the one who is in heaven" (Mt. 23:9). This remark of Jesus militates against a patriarchal interpretation of religious authority and rejects the idea of an immediate relationship between "earthly" and "heavenly" fatherhood. The experience of God and of his lordship, which Jesus wishes all who follow him to have, does not correspond to the process of the natural experience of father or to the structures of public order based on it. For anyone who does not "leave" father and mother, indeed, anyone who does not "hate" them, cannot enter into discipleship. Discipleship does not restore patriarchal "peace" but brings the "sword," the estrangement of the son from the father (Mt. 10:34f).

Nor is the Pauline and Johannine understanding of God and of his lordship oriented to the primary natural analogue, i.e., to birth. Paul and John understand God's lordship in terms of "new birth" and "rebirth." The experience of God revealed in Jesus is not simply a projection and extrapolation of the natural experience of a father. In Pauline terms, fatherhood is not to be determined by categories of the "flesh" but by categories of the "spirit." It is in this "spirit" that we cry "Abba, Father!" (Rom. 8:15).

It is precisely our confusion of the religious idea of God's lordship with the patriarchal authority of the father and the fact that in our times a universal patriarchal experience of order no longer exists that makes it so difficult for us to pray to God. Furthermore, the Church in exercising its pastoral authority often aggravates this situation by assuming the identification of divine lordship and patriarchal authority in situations where patriarchal authority no longer functions. The very image of God that confronts us in the life and message of Jesus himself is, however, the destruction of this identification. Therefore, the destruction of this relationship is not primarily the result of the social-psychological criticism of ideology and religion.

Jesus himself substitutes an historical experience of freedom for the natural experiences of man. He emancipates our religious experiences from the notion of an inevitably enveloping "natural order." He makes the experience of God primarily an experience of freedom. In this experience "we must become as little children," because we understand this freedom as a freedom for which we are grateful. It is a freedom that can never rid itself of the painful tension between emancipation and reconciliation. It is a freedom which recognizes that in its most important task it is dependent on forbearance. Here the possibility of experiencing a comforting and accessible God exists. Here we do not simply resign ourselves to the existing injustices and sufferings which ultimately become burdens for others. Rather we try to change injustice and suffering in order to experience them as not being everything there is to life. Thus, our name for God is not merely a cover-up for an anonymous fate, for the fate of a new "nature" in which man's as yet unrealized hopes ultimately disappear. In an age that only promises to increase the tragedies of the modern history of freedom and the tremendous suffering that men inflict on one another, is it possible to make credible a patriarchal concept of God grounded on the purely psychological archetype? To consider this matter and to create a conscious awareness of it seems to me to be one of the more important tasks facing the Church today.

A critical and liberating demolition of the patriarchal view of church authority is, of course, very closely connected to the issue of a patriarchal conception of God. The patriarchal view of church authority bears the marks of a religious projection of patriarchal notions of order even more clearly than does the idea of God as father. The patriarchal view of church authority is thus more and more open to the suspicion that it is "ideological." From a psychological, pastoral point of view this patriarchal view greatly hinders the concrete effectiveness and attractiveness of church authority and leads, both on the side of authority and on that of obedience, to empty forms of behavior. Where the Church maintains its patriarchal view of authority in spite of its own conscious or unconscious awareness of the emptiness of such a view, it provokes dependent behavior. It can also create anxiety among those who exercise authority, and this bodes no good for the future since anxious men can hardly lead in a spirit of freedom. What is needed, therefore, is not a restoration of authority after the image of a father—since a father, "because of the structure of society, can no longer maintain the ruling 'potestas' that conservative fantasy wishes to accord him."[6] Rather, the church should develop and again lend dignity to that dimension of its understanding of authority that is also central in its biblical foundation: namely, the authority of witness.

The authority of witness does not in itself exclude the institutional-representative element. The authority of witness does, however, link the institutional element directly to the fundamentals of "ethical authority." Rather than the image of father and the image of "pater," the images of witness and martyrdom must become regulative images for the understanding of church authority. In the Johannine tradition, for which the idea of witness and testimony is central, the origin of the Church's understanding of authority is clearly seen to be one of the authority of witness. An authority of witness clearly refers ecclesiastical forms of authority back to the authority of Jesus himself who, through the testimony he offered when he gave himself up to die on the cross, reveals and validates the tradition of freedom grounded in him.

▼

"From patriarchal authority to the authority of witness"—one should not underestimate the change this implies for the norms of the ecclesiastical exercise of authority. It decisively binds the practical understanding of church authority and church office to the Church's enduring witness and to the whole of the Church as a "pilgrim people of God." The recent council emphasized this new view of authority in order to define the meaning and function of church leadership as testimony. This new view of how authority should be reformed is likewise one of the starting points for the necessary confrontation between the Church's practical understanding of ecclesiastical authority and the modern history of freedom.

2. I have already spoken about the concrete confrontation of the Church with the modern history of freedom. Will the Church accept the challenge of this confrontation and build the new traditions that alone will permit old ones to remain alive? The mere preservation of tradition without the addition of new ones would be pure traditionalism. Traditionalism could never be a theological characteristic of the missionary Church of Jesus Christ; traditionalism is a characteristic of the *sect*. This gives us a catchword for what will occupy us in this second orientation: namely, the danger of sectarianism.

Whenever the Church does not face up to the challenges of the modern history of freedom, it runs the risk of itself becoming a sect, and thus losing its identity. The Church, as Church of the Son, cannot preserve its identity by cutting itself off from the "strangeness" of the historical world. It is the characteristic mark of the Church that it cannot possess its identity simply by the pure reproduction of its own traditions. Its founding began when the distinction between Jews and Gentiles ceased, when the Temple veil was torn and when the synagogue became a church for all people. Involvement in the "strange and foreign" became obligatory. From the beginning—and not just from the time of Constantine—the Church in an act of self-abrogation crossed over into that strange world to which it must constantly relate. It is the Church of the Son who reclaimed this "foreignness" as his own "property" and who sealed this claim with his death for *all* men—and this includes the nonbeliever, as an ancient church document already emphasized.[7]

Furthermore, this orientation to the "foreign" does not enter the Church as an afterthought. It is an element of its very constitution; it belongs to the Church's specific essence. The Church cannot know with certainty what is "humane" or what is and can be "Christlike" without the experiment of historical experience and dialogue. When the Church forgets this, or anxiously suppresses it, then the Church universal stands in danger of losing its identity and becoming a sect. Thus, when I speak here of the risk of sectarianism, I am not speaking sociologically or psychologically. I do not primarily mean that the Church becomes increasingly sectarian because of its minority status. Rather, I am referring to the theological sectarianism that so often characterizes the mentality that prevails within the Church.

Now, naturally, any talk about the danger of sectarianism requires a more careful explanation. First, I would like to make two general observations. One of them will help avoid a misunderstanding that could easily arise in light of the actual situation of the Catholic church after the latest council. Our diagnosis of the risk of sectarianism in the Church could be denied by arguing that today another countervailing danger threatens the Church even more. This danger arises from attempts at "reform" which are frequently proclaimed and undertaken in the interest of an uncritical and excessive "opening to the world." In these attempts the Church, its message, its structure and lifestyles are accommodated to the existing structures of our contemporary world and its forms of consciousness. Such attempts, it is argued, seem to introduce a sellout of traditional content and conviction and a loss of identity through accommodation.

Now I would not wish either to deny or to underestimate this danger. This danger is often caused by an all too one-dimensional and uninformed view of the Church's present situation, a view that generally operates with the same abstract view of the "Church and world" as held by conservatives. The only difference is that, unlike the conservative usage, it places the accent on "world" rather than "Church" and thus in its turn argues and reacts in dangerous clichés.

Nonetheless, it seems to me that this danger is less a cause than a symptom of the Church's current identity crisis. This becomes clear if one considers the present ecclesiastical situation not only in terms of the last ten years but also in terms of the whole history of freedom and enlightenment. This history continues to determine our present situation and makes it possible to give a definite meaning to the notion "world" in any discussion about the Church's relationship to it. From this point of view there is, in my opinion, a definite sectarian tendency in the Church and the beginning of a sectarian mentality. This fight against one-sided and over-simplified tendencies to accommodation in the Church's present situation reinforces this sectarian mentality.

My second observation is that we have no uniform theological standard to which to refer for the theological use we want to make of the term *sect*. In ordinary theological vernacular the word *sect* is in no way a refined ecclesiological category. It serves rather as a negative characterization of nonecclesiastical religious groups and mentalities. But this meaning of *sect* as it applies to confessions and religious groups in an ecclesiastical sense is not relevant to the ecclesiastical phenomenon we are speaking about. To be sure, modern sociology of religion has relativized the opposition between Church and sect that classical religious sociology presumed. To a certain extent the sociology of religion has brought about a gradual blending and relationship between these two ideas. However, the issue that concerns us is not a sociological but a theological description and evaluation of certain trends in the Church's present situation. Thus, the discussion here is explicitly about the *danger* of an ecclesiastical sectarian mentality! It is of value first of all to describe some of the symptoms of this mentality. In doing this we will not be considering the positive senses in which the word *sect* could be used: for example, the sect as an eschatologically motivated reform or "underground" movement, or as a form of organization for a charismatic and critical avant-garde, etc. (For this positive understanding of sects there are parallels in the non-ecclesiastical and nonreligious sector, as in political or social sects.) Hence, in using the concept *sect*, we have in mind the negative meaning.

a. As a general symptom of this sectarian mentality that implicitly includes the other symptoms, I would just like to mention the confusion of the "noncontemporaneity" (Ungleichzeitigkeit) of ecclesiastical forms of life with the "untimeliness" (Unzeitgemäss-heit) of the Christian message; or, to put it another way, the confusion of "noncontemporaneity" with the conscious adherence to noncontemporary forms of consciousness based on an appeal to the untimeliness of the content of the Christian faith. This confusion has grave consequences. "Noncontemporaneity" is one thing. "Untimeliness" is another. The message of redemption in the cross of Jesus Christ is in fact untimely, inopportune, and it will always remain so. But there is also an odd kind of irrelevance or noncontemporaneity. In many forms of the Church's consciousness and proclamation a certain "out-of-touch-ness" with contemporary social, political, and cultural issues that are the product of the modern history of freedom and enlightenment is evident. Is it not precisely this peculiar noncontemporaneity that keeps the Church from making effective in a convincing and liberating way the essential untimeliness of the memory of Jesus Christ that it transmits and makes public?

Actually it seems to me that an irrelevant and noncontemporaneous religion in fact succumbs to accommodation, and by this accommodation to stagnation! There is nothing courageous in such a religion, nothing liberating or redemptive. For where religion and the Church in their views, life-styles, and structures function in a manner irrelevant to the problems and structures of contemporary society, there the challenging "untimeliness" and "foreignness" of their proclamation can be judged as outdated and can be all too easily dismissed. In such situations, the "untimeliness" of the gospel can be construed as a sign that the Church itself is irrelevant and represents an anachronistic state of social development and general awareness.

Who can deny that much of what is expressed from the pulpit as the "paradox" or the "scandal" of Christianity, as the contradiction or strangeness of the cross, merely serves as evidence of an irrelevant awareness and not as evidence of the untimeliness of the folly of the cross? This "noncontemporaneity" makes it more difficult for many people to see the relevance of the Church's proclamation to their lives, their fears, and their hopes. Accordingly, their vital identification with the Church dwindles. The number of those who feel themselves to be a part of the Church becomes smaller and smaller—despite all the talk about the importance of the laity in the Church.

There are those who attempt to put the blame for this desperate situation on people who have difficulty identifying with the Church. These make quick reference to the Church as a "small flock," and speak in the present critical situation about a "healthy reduction" in church membership. But this attitude of accusation only fosters the sectarian fate of the Church and avoids the painful task of overcoming the Church's meaninglessness.

b. Another symptom of sectarianism is a growing inability or unwillingness to undergo new experiences and then to consider and critically assimilate them into the self-understanding of faith, Church and theology. Here a particular atrophy arises in the Church's critical power of assimilation. The danger in this seems obvious to me. Precisely in order to preserve its apostolic tradition, the Church is compelled to undergo new experiences and renew itself out of the ferment of what is unconquered in the alien world that surrounds it. The Church is compelled painstakingly to assimilate these new experiences. If it wants to limit itself to the reproduction of its own traditions, it will finally lose them altogether. If the Church is no longer ready to undergo new experiences and to assimilate a new historical epoch into the horizon of faith, it will ultimately forget the message it is called to remember, for the Church's task is to transmit publicly a courageous memory that tries to speak to the future of every person.

In this context I might make mention of a dangerous mechanism operative in the way many ecclesiastical authorities assert themselves in the face of new questions and challenges. It is the tendency to wait until newly raised questions and problems (the charisma of freedom, a new public image, the call to social involvement, etc.) have become slogans. Of course, frustrated questions degenerate very quickly into exaggeration and over-simplification—into slogans and jargon. The Church then exposes them as slogans, while the actual challenges these problems pose are effectively avoided.

A similar mechanism seems to arise in the confrontation with the modern history of freedom. Unsolved questions are answered by trying to relativize them historically, as in this manner: "Oh, that's just the Enlightenment!" or "But Marx and Nietzsche have already said that!"—the assumption being that something is actually solved in this way. The anonymous pressure of these problems, however, remains and grows, and like ghosts these questions always come back to haunt our ecclesiastical and theological consciousness. Thus a dangerous vacuum is formed in the Church's public image into which other forces and substitute solutions are drawn.

What does this imply for the Church today? In my judgment it implies at least the following. The Church ought to direct its attention to a catalogue of suppressed problems and questions. Only in this way can we satisfy those who raise critical questions while exercising their critical freedom. Only thus can we overcome a nervous escalation of criticism in the Church. Only thus will the capacity of identifying with the Church avoid further weakening. And only thus can new experiences find a home in the Church. Without them the Church runs the risk of losing the convincing force of its old traditions as well.

c. The sectarian mentality can also be found in the attempt to ascribe the unrest aroused by critical freedom in the Church exclusively to sociological and psychological factors. Once again this avoids confronting the modern history of freedom, which is penetrating willy-nilly into the Church. Accordingly, the Church maintains her structure without the public presence of a mature freedom. To develop a culture of freedom and an habitual maturity in the Church would be no mean pastoral task. It ought to be as much the object of persistent effort as the attempt to move from freedom that is polemical and ideal to freedom that is structured and real. This is so not in spite of but because of the fact that the mark of the church community is love.

There is also another mechanism operative in the Church in which the sectarian mentality seems to me to be secretly at work. This occurs when the call for democratization of ecclesiastical structures and life-styles—a call which admittedly is often issued crudely and thoughtlessly—is met with the argument that the Church is ultimately a voluntary association of members from which, in contrast to a natural society, a member can withdraw if he does not agree with its existing structures and practices. Yet on the basis of such an argument every change in ecclesiastical structures and life-styles can ultimately be stopped. Furthermore, changes that take place in the Church can no longer be explained. In addition, this argumentation taken in itself threatens to isolate the Church and its structures so much from the modern social and political processes of freedom that the Church nearly becomes an ecclesiological counterideology to the idea of democratization. Such a counterideology can be criticized as a symptom of the Church's sectarian mentality—even if one agrees only in part that the Church should accept democratic models and methods as normative for itself.

d. I could go on to cite many other symptoms of the sectarian mentality in the Church. However, I will mention only a few. The danger of sectarian mentality appears in a more strictly theological way, in my opinion, in the notion of a "pure theology," a new elitist gnosis that articulates the aristocratic side of the sectarian mentality. It prizes the arcanum, in which it protects more the spirit of Plato than the spirit of Christ. Yet the spirit of Christ knows quite well, in the sovereignty of its love, how to protect itself from "profanation" without thereby ceasing to be an inexhaustible offer of salvation to everyone, especially to "those on the outside." Finally, there is a special kind of sectarian mentality that is revealed in the manner in which we still all calmly and passively accept the scandal of division in modern Christianity.

Hopefully these observations have clarified somewhat what I see as "the risk of sectarianism." As I understand it, becoming a sect is not the right path for the Church to follow in its quest for identity. In my judgment this road leads the Church astray. There are some who argue for a restoration of the situation of the primitive Church. Much could be said against them, but I mention only the following: neither the pre-Constantinian Church nor the Church of the Roman community were ever sects in the theological sense outlined above. The early Church resisted the invitation to become one of the various national sects in the Roman Empire, and by this resistance finally destroyed the ancient cult of the emperors and inaugurated a new situation of freedom. The Church recognized no isolating "divine barrier" between itself and the surrounding world of Hellenistic culture. It knew that its own identity was indeterminate and open for the sake of its obligation to witness to

that freedom which was set free in the Son. The Church knew that
as the Church of the crucified Son it could not accommodate itself
to existing forms of consciousness and existing perceptions of the
world. In addition it knew that it could not allow itself to be assimilated by these influences without a struggle. As "a holy remnant"
the Church knew that it had taken upon itself the inviolability and
untimeliness of its messages. For the church understood that the
distance and strangeness from the world characteristic of Jesus'
message was not the same as sectarian isolation from the world.

Nonetheless, if I am not mistaken, a truly sectarian mentality is
spreading in the Church. This threat is not infrequently found in
those circles that never tire of proclaiming their "orthodoxy" and
loyalty to the Church. This is destined, however, to undermine
church authority rather than preserve it. Thus the phrase "discern-
ment of spirits"—a phrase which the Church eagerly uses against
others—must also be applied to itself. Naturally nothing is accomplished by biting arguments and counterarguments, for these are in
themselves clearly symptomatic of the sectarian mentality! However,
the complexity and distress of today's ecclesiastical situation should
not be underestimated. The temptation of defining itself as a sect
is close at hand within the Church, for it is true that a carelessly
pursued "openness" to a world upon whose formation the Church
can exercise no more influence leads to an accommodation that
is essentially legitimation. It leads to a surrender of the Church
and of her inherited traditions to the prevailing forms of thought
and life. In reaction to this danger those who wish to protect the
authenticity of the Church's missions and of the message it transmits can easily find themselves tempted to close off the Church, to
shield it from the challenges of the world. But the transmitted content of the Christian message does not permit this. It is precisely
this very content, these very traditions, that forbid the Church to
transmit its message to itself alone. They forbid the Church to
isolate itself from the "strange" and the "new" in the world. Would
not this kind of sectlike self-isolation be only another form of self-
annihilation by accommodation? Accordingly, I would like to
articulate the following pastoral and theological task for the Church
today: *the preservation of church consciousness from an increasing
sect-mentality*.

This task is not guided by the conservative expectation of a new "world Church" in the society of the future. It does not tacitly presuppose the idea of a Christian culture in order then to describe present-day dissocialization and isolation as "sectarian." Nor does the task demand a blind denial of the minority status that sociology predicts for tomorrow's Church. It demands only the contravention of the sectarian fate that threatens the Church from within. For it is not minority status but a certain mentality which defines a sect in the theological sense.

The Church of Christ ought neither to fear minority status nor be ashamed of it. Such fear or shame comes from viewing the Church as the this-worldly executrix of the universal history of salvation to which the Church itself bears witness. But this is to misunderstand salvation-history as a religious philosophy of history instead of as the Church's own hope. What the Church must fear, however, is the creeping sectarian mentality described above.

Preservation of church consciousness from the sect mentality—that seems to me to be a task which the coming synod owes to its pastoral concern. It is a task owed to all who have remained loyal, but also to those who have recently turned themselves from the church. Above all, it is a task owed to the responsible confession of the message of Jesus himself. For how could a Church which became a sect in the theological sense still be the Church of Jesus Christ? It would be the completely assimilated religion of a secularized society. Ultimately what remains is the dead, stifled residue of a hope that was once vital and courageous and liberating for all, a hope to which there is no alternative either purely within the history of attempts to create freedom or purely outside of (i.e., in isolation from) that history.

The Dangerous Memory of the Freedom of Jesus*

The Church must understand and confirm her existence in the midst of our so-called progressive society as the witness to and bearer of a dangerous memory of freedom. The Church lives from memory (*memoria*), which is a basic way of expressing Christian

* Professor Metz has suggested that this portion of his *Concilium* Congress lecture be added as the final section of this chapter.

faith. It lives from the specific meaning of freedom at the heart of this faith.

We Christians live out of the memory of the suffering, death, and resurrection of Jesus Christ. When we believe in him, we remember the testament of his love. In his love, the sovereignty of God came into the world as an act challenging man's domination over man. Jesus challenged man's domination over man when he identified himself with unreserved love with those who were being oppressed. His loving identification with the insignificant, rejected, and oppressed expressed God's sovereignty and was an act of liberation. For us to remember Jesus in this way is, therefore, not to evade, but to face the risks of the future. Such a memory contains a definite anticipation of the future as a future for the hopeless, broken, and oppressed. For this reason, it is a dangerous and liberating memory which puts pressure on our present lives, calling them into question.

The Christian hopes not in just any open future, but precisely in that future which is shaped by God's sovereignty and brings justice to the oppressed. Our memory of Jesus constantly forces us to transform ourselves in order to do justice to this future. This memory breaks through the structures of the dominant consciousness of our age, a one-dimensional way of looking at things which hides the fact of oppression and injustice from us. It mobilizes tradition as a dangerous tradition and thus as a critical and liberating power opposed to the security of those "whose hour is always there" (Jn. 7:6). It repeatedly raises the suspicion that the so-called "plausibility structures" of a society (P. Berger) may well be "structures of delusion" (K. Marx). It refuses to measure the relevance of its critique on what "a somewhat sleepy, elderly businessman after lunch" holds to be self-evident and relevant.

In my opinion, Christian faith must be seen as a memory subversive of such kinds of "self-evidence" and "relevance." The Church is the public form of this memory. Hence, the Church's beliefs and affirmations should be formulas in which this dangerous memory is spelled out in a public way. The criterion of their being genuinely Christian is precisely in their *dangerousness,* in their freeing and saving power as they recall the freedom of Jesus and his unreserved love for the oppressed.

The Church is the public memory of the freedom of Jesus and also the proclaimer of a freedom that is still coming to man. This freedom is God's eschatological history of liberation, constituted in the cross and resurrection of Jesus. This *eschatological* history of liberation cannot be dissolved into the ideal of a *revolutionary* history of liberation, nor is it identical with the *liberal* history of enlightenment. Nonetheless, it does accept responsibility for the historical realization of freedom: "For all things are yours, whether Paul or Apollos or Cephas, or the world or life or death, or things present or things to come. All things are yours; and you are Christ's; and Christ is God's." (I Cor. 3:21-23.)

The memory of the freedom of Jesus is, in this sense, an emancipatory memory which frees from every idolizing or absolutizing of cosmic and political powers. In its light, all political orders are essentially constituted by human freedom. In its light, the political ethos of the pre-established order is transformed into a political ethos of change and transformation by freedom. The things that lie beyond the range of human freedom and its conflicts—consummation, reconciliation, and peace—are reserved to God and the "not-yet" by virtue of the "eschatological proviso." For this reason, the church must bring all its critical power to bear upon totalitarian systems and ideologies that promote "one-dimensional emancipation."

Wherever the eschatological character of freedom is forgotten and the history of freedom is regarded as completed and fulfilled, "freedom" becomes an idea which justifies the totalitarian domination of one man, class, race, nation, or group over another. Wherever the eschatological character of freedom is forgotten, we fall into the danger of identifying an inner-worldly development or triumph with the whole history of freedom. Whenever the history of freedom loses its eschatological remembrance, it neglects the new conflicts and catastrophes that originate in the freedom man has already gained, and it interprets the prior sufferings of man as merely the "prehistory of freedom."

But where is this eschatological memory of freedom alive and effective? Where is it calling into question the cognitive and affective systems of our "progressive" societies? Who can lead us to the freedom that is so often forgotten or suppressed, to the freedom to suffer from the sufferings of others and to heed the prophecy of their suffering (even though the fact of suffering seems to have become socially "improper")? Who can lead us to the freedom to become old, especially in a society that seems to be defined by its denial of age and by its secret shame of aging? Who can lead us to the freedom of contemplation, even though we seem to be hypnotized by work, achievement, and planning right into the deepest chambers of our consciousness? Who responds to cries for freedom in past sufferings and hopes? Who answers the challenge of the dead and makes conscience sensitive to their freedom? Who cultivates solidarity with the dead to whom we ourselves shall belong the day after tomorrow? And finally, who can share his understanding of freedom with those who are ground down and die under the banalities of everyday life, those whose deaths are less dramatic, though no less real, than the martyr-soldiers who fall on the battlefront of revolutions for liberation?

Who insists on all these dimensions of our history of freedom? A society that ignores or suppresses these dimensions pays for this through the growing loss of its sensitivity to freedom itself. The eschaton of such a society is boredom. Its myth is credulous trust in total planning. The concealed interest that directs its ideology is the abolition of all risk in the world, so as not to feel its challenges any longer. Thus it is that we have "in Western society, a patronizing pluralistic boredom and, in communist societies, a commanded and forced monolithic boredom. . . . Things look as they do when there is a partial eclipse of the sun. Everything is so remarkably gray. The birds either don't sing or do so in a different way. Something is wrong in such a world. All the intimations of transcendence are weakened" (E. Bloch). In other words, the dangerous memory seems to be quenched; the eschatological remembrance has fallen still.

Has Christianity failed historically? Has the Church abdicated historical responsibility for this memory? Can one now define the future of human freedom only in terms of secular symbols and utopias? The general judgment from outside the Church (and sometimes also within it) seems to hold this view. In modern social theories, the classical critique of religion concentrated first of all on the Church itself. It usually characterized the Church as an organization of non-contemporary consciousness, as an institutionalized ostracizing of knowing and productive curiosity. It regarded the Church as an anti-emancipatory remnant of the past, whose interest in human freedom and rectitude was merely simulated. The Church was seen as offering only a narcotic for painful and unjust situations.

Recently, modern social theories have spoken of a growing lack of function of the Church in modern society. Hence, the earlier sharp criticism of the Church has increasingly softened into indifference or benevolent politeness—a compassion like that traditionally extended to the dying. Even militant communists are increasingly curbing themselves in their fight against a totally privatized Church. And in Western futurologies, the Church is seldom mentioned or discussed only as a negligible factor. Liberal Christians also assert an irreversible "departure from the churches" and recommend an eclectic cult-Christianity as therapeutic relief from the coercive mechanism of society.

Are all these judgments no more than modern clichés? Are they only prejudiced and one-sided opinions? Do they simply illustrate the fact that the Church continues to be under attack in the world today as yesterday, that is, continues to be in that agonizing situation of the community of a crucified Lord with which every believer must soberly reckon? I believe that this specifically theological answer should not be given too quickly. To give this answer would be to overlook a profound reason for this predominant modern attitude towards the Church, namely, the disappointing historical experience that has been had with the Church.

Modern man recollects so many historical disappointments. He is aware of generations of suspect ecclesiastical alliances with the ruling powers. He has the confusing impression of the Church as a religion that no longer believes in its own hope, but only in its institutional reproduction. We must take these recollections into account. They are more indelible than we might like to suppose. If we are to make the Church credible, we must confront this suspicious memory rather than seek to vindicate the church's original foundation and apostolic succession. To confront this suspicious memory: that is the crucial historical-hermeneutical problem that our understanding of the Church faces today. And we cannot solve this problem by giving "better" or "more subtle" interpretations of the Church's history. We can only solve it by a new practice, a painful transformation, a "proof of the spirit and power." It is here that all church reform is rooted.

This practical proof is not at all concerned with a cheap modernization for the Church, but with its historical identity, continuity, and mission. This practical proof of the Church, this painful transformation and bearing of the spirit and power, is given through *us*. We must be it; we ourselves, we Christians, we who seek to live from the memory of Jesus Christ, we for whom the idea of a completely institution-free and churchless handing on of this memory appears as the illusion of a totally privatized faith.

NOTES

1. Johann Baptist Metz, "The Responsibility of Hope," *Philosophy Today X* (1966) 287.

2. An introductory section of Metz's essay, as well as a number of other sentences, have been omitted from this English translation since they refer specifically to current events in Germany at the time the essay was being written. Chief of these is Professor Metz's references to an imminent pastoral synod. At certain other points where Metz speaks of the "synod's task," the reference has been rendered in a general way as the "Church's task."

3. The term "practical-critical" derives from the Enlightenment, especially from the philosophy of Kant. In Kant, the Enlightenment sought to define its own limitations. Hence, Kant's philosophy came to be known as the critical philosophy. The early Enlightenment had championed scientific knowledge as the source of man's freedom and regeneration; and "science" meant the use of mathematical reason in man's attempt to control and dominate nature. But Kant, contravening the early Enlightenment, perceived that a blind faith in reason, at least scientifically conceived, would issue in the imprisonment rather than further liberation of man. Man would, he felt, be seen and eventually dealt with as an object among other objects in a world conceived as a closed system of causal connections (Newton, Locke, Hume). Or he would be imprisoned by new metaphysical and dogmatic mystifications (Spinoza, Leibnitz, and Wolff).

Accordingly, Kant, although believing with the early Enlightenment (Newton, Locke, Hume, Spinoza, Leibnitz, and Wolff) in the primacy of reason, transformed the concept of reason. He did so by broadening the concept of reason to include more than the scientific and theoretical use of it. Following the suggestions of Jean-Jacques Rousseau, Kant ascribed a dual function to reason, arguing that the scientific function of reason can be put to an empirical use alone; and that the primary function of reason as the source of freedom and truth is operative in the practical life of man, that is in the sphere of moral action and actuation of moral goals. In this way Kant claimed to have established a practical-critical philosophy: critical, because it challenged the universalization of a specifically scientific reason, and practical, because it placed primacy upon the attainment of freedom for man in moral practice and willing.

What is crucial here is the understanding of reason as a self-determining ground of being. For Kant, rationality and freedom are present and attained in the realization of *willed* relationships and goals. Irrationality is eliminated from the life of man through moral action and not by scientific knowledge alone. "Practical-critical" refers to this dimension of human life.

4. One of the central notions of Metz's essay is the complex concept suggested by the German compound "Freiheitsgeschichte." In the English we have used "the modern history of freedom" and similar variant phrases to translate this word which means, literally, "freedom-history."

When English-speaking peoples think of the history of freedom, they turn habitually to the story of the events by which man's political structures have become more free and democratic. They think of the French and American Revolutions, the Magna Carta, the Declaration of Independence, the Bill of Rights, and the Constitution. Events such as these, landmarks in man's political "progress," are included in Metz's thought when he speaks of the "modern history of freedom." In addition, Metz has in mind the history of the Marxist revolutions, and in this aspect he illustrates his dependence upon the Marxist-Christian dialogue.

5. Ernst Käsemann, *Jesus Means Freedom* (Philadelphia: Fortress, 1970), p. 42.

6. A. Mitscherlich, *Auf dem Weg zur Vaterlose Gesellschaft,* (Munich: Piper, 1963), p. 296.

7. *Denzinger* 1294; also 1096.

74 75 76 77 10 9 8 7 6 5 4 3 2 1